MW00834391

# The End

## from

# the Beginning

## THE APOCALYPTIC VISION
## OF ISAIAH

Avraham Gileadi

HEBRAEUS PRESS

The End from the Beginning
© Copyright 1997 by Avraham Gileadi
All rights Reserved
Published in the United States of America
Second Edition, First Printing, April 1997

No part of this work may be reproduced in any manner whatso-
ever without written permission from the publisher, Hebraeus
Press, P.O. Box 183, Cave Junction, OR 97523.

This work does not represent the views of any religion, church, or
sect but is the responsibility solely of the author.

ISBN 0-910511-01-2

# The End

## from

# the Beginning

*"I foretell the end from the beginning,
from ancient times things not yet done."*
                                                    –Isaiah 46:10

# Contents

INTRODUCTION ................................................................. 1
  Contemporary Views on Ancient Writings ........................... 2
  Evidence for a Single Author of Isaiah ............................... 4
  Overlooked Themes and Theologies .................................... 8
  A Complex Message Made Simple ...................................... 10

CHAPTER 1 — VISIONS OF THE END OF THE WORLD ........... 13
  The Pattern of Hebrew Prophecy ....................................... 14
  The Prophetic Pattern in Israel's History ............................. 16
  Ancient Names as Codenames ........................................... 20
  Types for a Future Worldwide Judgment .............................. 23

CHAPTER 2 — MESSAGES CONCEALED IN FORM
  AND STRUCTURE ......................................................... 27
  Structure and Content–Two Dimensions .............................. 29
  Trouble at Home, Exile Abroad, Happy Homecoming .................. 30
  A Distinction between Prophecy and History .......................... 32
  Apostasy, Judgment, Restoration, Salvation .......................... 34
  Threat One, Threat Two, Threat Three ................................. 36
  The Curses and the Blessings ........................................... 37
  Destruction of the Wicked/Deliverance of the Righteous ............. 39
  Isaiah's Structures Reveal a Divine Plan .............................. 41

CHAPTER 3 — THE RECYCLING OF HISTORY ............................43
   The Past Foreshadows the Future........................................44
   A Future Chronology of Past Events.................................46
   Doomsday for the Wicked ....................................................49
   Millennial Peace for the Righteous ..................................52
   What Has Been Shall Be Again ...........................................55

CHAPTER 4 — THE COVENANT WITH ISRAEL ...........................57
   Two Types of Covenants .......................................................57
   The Meaning of Covenant Making .....................................59
   Israel Is Responsible for Herself ......................................62
   The Role of the King in Israel .............................................64
   God's Covenant with David .................................................66
   God Makes a New Covenant ................................................69

CHAPTER 5 — ZION AND BABYLON IDEOLOGIES ..................71
   Isaiah's Seven-Part Structure ...............................................72
   A Prophecy and a Theology..................................................74
   Ruin and Rebirth.....................................................................76
   Rebellion and Compliance ...................................................76
   Punishment and Deliverance................................................77
   Humiliation and Exaltation ..................................................77
   Suffering and Salvation.........................................................78
   Disloyalty and Loyalty..........................................................79
   Disinheritance and Inheritance...........................................80
   Structures Determine Time Frames.....................................81
   Zion and Babylon as Archetypes........................................84

CHAPTER 6 — THE TYRANT AND THE SERVANT ......................87
   The Tyrant Conquers the World...........................................88
   Personifications in Metaphor................................................92
   The Servant Has Many Types...............................................96
   Jewish Messianic Expectations............................................100

CHAPTER 7 — THE LADDER TO HEAVEN..............................101
   Isaiah–Prophet and Theologian .........................................102
   An Ascending and Descending Order............................103
   Passing the Tests of God....................................................105
   Living Role Models.............................................................108
   Unimpeded Progress Upward...........................................112
   Descent before Ascent .......................................................114

CHAPTER 8 — THE SAVIOR-GOD OF ISRAEL .........................117
   God Is Bound by Covenant Relationships ......................118
   Death, the Common Enemy ..............................................121
   God, Our Proxy, Overcomes Death..................................124
   A Reversal of Circumstances at the End of the World................129

CHAPTER 9 — THE END FROM THE BEGINNING .................131
   A Polarization of All People ..............................................132
   The Literal Fulfillment of Prophecy.................................134
   Righteousness Precedes Salvation....................................136
   Distinct Roles of Men and Women...................................140
   A Brief Warning before the End .......................................143

KEY WORDS ................................................................147

# Introduction

For as long as I can remember, I have been fascinated by biblical prophecy. It seemed like proof to me of the existence of God. As a child in Europe during World War II, I had seen cities burn, warplanes crash, people evacuated. I had lived with scarcity and felt fear all around me. Yet I felt there had to be a redeeming factor to this life. Prophecy confirmed that feeling of hope no matter what else might happen.

In particular, the books of the prophets seemed to answer so many questions about current world events. I felt inside that the ancient prophets were speaking about our time as well as theirs. No one had to tell me this; I just "knew" it. And yet, reading the writings of the prophets was like reading sealed books. I wanted to know what key unlocked their meaning so that there could be no doubt about how to interpret them.

## Contemporary Views on Ancient Writings

As I grew up and looked into various religions, I found that not all readers of the prophets felt as I did. Some Christians believed that Hebrew prophecy relates to modern times, that history repeats itself, and that the things the prophets predicted for ancient times could happen again. Judaism, I learned, teaches that the writings of the prophets may be read on two distinct levels: one relating to a prophet's own day, to events in his time; the other applying to the end of the world. Conditions at that time would so resemble those in the prophet's day that his prophecy would have a second fulfillment.

However, these views fell flat with most other religionists. Nearly all modern Bible scholars, for example, viewed Hebrew prophecy as firmly grounded in the prophets' own era. They felt that there existed no proof that the prophets spoke about anything other than their own day.

So as a young man, I studied the Hebrew Bible in a rabbinic school. There I began to understand the Jewish method of interpreting a single verse of prophecy on many levels—literal, allegorical, historical, typological. I pored over Jewish commentaries of the Bible and sat with rabbis who unfolded the various ways of interpreting the prophets. I also went to college and learned that prophets were poets as well as men of God. They organized their writings so that their literary features, too, possessed a meaning. Every word meant something by how it was placed as well as by what it said.

Yet neither rabbinic school nor college seemed to have enough answers. Did or didn't the prophets speak of our day? The rabbis really believed we were living in the time spoken of by the prophets, but they couldn't provide the proof I was looking for. They were interpreters of the scriptures, not literary scholars. The scholars, meanwhile, would come close to capturing the meaning of a prophet's thought, but then, refusing to believe that someone could know the future, they would explain it away. Just when I believed we were onto something important that appeared to relate a prophecy to our day, it would be blown away like the smoke of their cigars.

I also found out that the scholarly world is filled with enmity and academic envy. Liberal scholars of the Bible—whose positions on these questions were widely accepted and set in concrete—looked down on their conservative counterparts, sometimes refusing even to acknowledge them as scholars. Conservative scholars laughed at the shallow arguments of the liberals, viewing them as unbelievers who adopted their positions by common consent, not by an honest look at the evidence.

Of course there were always exceptions to the rule. In general, however, I found academia unfriendly to things of the spirit. So I held on to my feeling that the prophets were talking about our time while I did my best to learn the accepted viewpoints and repeat them back in the exams.

## Evidence for a Single Author of Isaiah

I attached myself to two Bible scholars, Dr. David Noel Freedman and Dr. R. K. Harrison, both of whom were honest and kind. One was liberal, the other conservative. I absorbed every positive thing they had to offer. From one I learned not to be daunted by the strength of numbers of an opposing point of view. Everything was open to investigation and subject to hard evidence, even things supposedly set in concrete. From the other I learned how to keep things simple. Creative, innovative research and evidence can be presented simply and convincingly on the most learned level of investigation.

Halfway into my doctoral program I finally had my breakthrough—a discovery in the prophetic books that helped me renew my quest for proof that the Hebrew prophets spoke of our day. It came when I was translating the Book of Isaiah from the Hebrew into modern English. I was hoping to publish my translation to show how Isaiah appears to reflect the socio-political condition of our modern world. I chose

Isaiah because of all Hebrew prophecy it has the most substance. It is the largest and most powerful book of prophecy in the Bible, and the most formidable. It also has been a particular point of controversy among scholars for decades.

While translating Isaiah, I discovered a series of verses in one part of the book that paralleled, verse by verse, in counterpoise, another such series in a different part of the book. Twenty-one consecutive verses in one location described a false god, the king of Babylon. These verses distinctly contrasted twenty-one verses in another location that described the God of Israel, the King of Zion. Most scholars had concluded that separate authors composed these different sections of the Book of Isaiah. Imagine my surprise, therefore, that two such different parts could be so closely related to one another.

The first series of these verses appears in chapter 14, in the first section of the Book of Isaiah. In that part, Israel still occupies her homeland, and God warns her that if she does not repent a world power from the North will invade and destroy and take people captive. Scholars say that Isaiah wrote this section himself. The other series of verses covers chapters 52-53, forming a part of that middle section of the book liberal scholars call Second Isaiah (assuming that an author other than Isaiah wrote it). That part of the book deals with Israel's exile among the nations of the world because of her wickedness. But she will return to the land—as the third and final section of the book predicts—in a future day of salvation.

The close interrelationship of two apparently unrelated parts of Isaiah suggested to me that a single author wrote both. Also, the verse-by-verse contrast of the God of Israel, the King of Zion, with a false god, the king of Babylon, meant that Isaiah had more in mind than actual events of his time. It meant he not only dealt with historical persons, but also with archetypes that transcend time and history and personify good or evil traits for all who read.

Here were two passages, separated far from each other, that described the character traits of one king as the opposite of the other. Scholars had long argued over the king of Babylon in chapter 14. Who was he? These contrasting verses promised to shed light on that question. In addition, these passages contained perhaps the best-known and most important messianic prophecy of all, that of the Suffering Servant in chapter 53. How could we understand about this "man of sorrows" without taking into account the full context of the prophecy provided by these matching verses? Somehow chapters 52 and 14 formed an integral part of what was prophesied in chapter 53.

It was evident to me that the author had composed two separate blocks of material so that they perfectly correlated. I was very excited about this discovery, but my college professors virtually dismissed it. They regarded it as a good beginning, that was all. I was told it takes ten years of full-time research to start to make a contribution in this field, and now, in retrospect, I agree with them. I had obtained my Master's degree only to realize I was not the master of anything. My doctoral chairman suggested Isaiah was too big for me to tackle, which made me rethink my whole position. If I wanted to narrow my focus to Isaiah, I would actually have to broaden my studies—and far more than I had anticipated.

So I began an intensive study of ancient Near Eastern history and texts. I discovered that Isaiah uses—and modifies—a variety of structures that appear in ancient Near Eastern literatures. Isaiah must have been well aware of the writings of the Egyptians, Canaanites, Babylonians, and Hittites, as he uses their literary patterns so adeptly. Because every structure conveys a message of its own, I realized that all these deserved to be explored.

I saw that the field of Bible studies was wide open for investigation and that to understand the Book of Isaiah, we need to understand the book's governing literary structures. Without that understanding, it would be like someone claiming to know the universe without ever having looked into space.

## Overlooked Themes and Theologies

I began to notice other things in the Book of Isaiah as well. Scholars often discussed parts of things while missing the whole. For example, some had noticed a new exodus theme: just as there occurred an exodus of the Israelites out of Egypt, so there would occur another miraculous exodus from all areas of the earth, wherever God had scattered Israel. However, scholars had not mentioned that the new exodus is one of an entire series of new events that Isaiah predicts. He links to this new exodus a new Passover, a new wandering in the wilderness, a new inheritance of the promised land, and many other new events. In fact, Isaiah uses every important event in Israel's past to prophesy Israel's future. History would repeat itself, and God would orchestrate it.

Similarly, scholars had discovered that the covenants ancient Near Eastern emperors made with their subservient or vassal kings and the covenants God had made with Israel and her kings resembled each other. God stood in the role of an emperor and the kings assumed the roles of vassals. Scholars also wrote that a vassal king could obtain or lose the emperor's protection, depending on the vassal's faithfulness to the emperor. If the vassal king kept the terms of the covenant, the emperor was duty bound to come to the aid of the king and his people when they were mortally threatened.

But scholars had never pinpointed the vassal king's role as that of a proxy protector. The emperor protected the people of the vassal king *for the sake of* the vassal king, not for the people's own sake. The vassal king, in other words, stood in for his people in obtaining the emperor's deliverance from any outside threat.

Scholars had also never applied the idea of such proxy protection to God's covenant with Israelite kings, only vaguely to vassal kings in general. Yet, the idea of proxy protection weaves itself throughout Christian theology. If you understand that idea, you will see the significance of the Messiah being a descendant of King David with whom God made such a covenant.

My confidence grew as I found these puzzle pieces and slowly put them together. I was a fairly novice scholar; could it be I was naive enough to see these things in a new light?

I also began to read apocalyptic works, which prophesy the end of the world. In that literature, I located the contrast between Zion and Babylon, the same as in Isaiah. Apocalyptic writers depict Zion as an archetype of good and Babylon as an archetype of evil. This was another clue to follow. Was there a provable relationship between Isaiah and endtime prophecy? I was determined to find out.

## A Complex Message Made Simple

For the next twenty years, the Book of Isaiah became my main area of study. Even my doctoral program fell far short of mastering this subject. Twenty years has only begun to show me what a wealth of divine knowledge is contained in just one book of Hebrew prophecy. Only a prophet of God—and an extraordinary poet—could have composed such a beautiful and intricate work as the Book of Isaiah.

In this simplified version of my work, I present my findings for the average reader of the Bible. I have met hundreds of such readers who have struggled with trying to understand Isaiah. Most begin with a deep love for Isaiah's poetry and an intuitive grasp of Isaiah's transcendent vision of both the terrors and glories of the earth's future. To all who love Hebrew prophecy I offer this book to guide you through much that is new and yet old, startling truths you may not have known were there.

I could not have written this version of Isaiah's message without first having completed a far more technical work—*The Literary Message of Isaiah.*[*] It examines the inner workings of the Book of Isaiah

---

[*] Copies of *The Literary Message of Isaiah* (New York: Hebraeus Press, 1994, 610 pp.) are available from Hebraeus Press, P. O. Box 183, Cave Junction, OR 97523. Please remit (U.S.) $25.00 plus $5.00 shipping ($10.00 shipping overseas). Expect delivery in two to four weeks stateside and two months overseas.

that scholars so often overlook when reading Hebrew prophecy: the sublime concepts that lie embedded within its literary features. Becoming familiar with the underlying structures of a book of prophecy–the configurations of themes, literary patterns, linking ideas, key words, etc.–a reader can better understand the message of what is being said on the surface.

After such close scrutiny of the Hebrew prophets, one begins to love the prophets themselves, and that is how I feel about Isaiah. Throughout Israel's history, we see God's love at work on behalf of his children. The Hebrew prophets were God's spokesmen to Israel and to all nations. If God's judgments upon Israel often seem harsh, that is because Israel kept faltering in her mission. The passages of condemnation of Israel are unsparing. Yet I believe that God's kindly, benevolent acts far surpass his divine chastisements of bad behavior.

In fact, the Book of Isaiah is a good example of God's benevolence in spite of his chastisements. Isaiah's prophecies more than balance the negative aspects of Israel's past with the bright destiny God reveals for her future. God offers so many blessings to his faithful people, then and now. His promises put in clear perspective our lives here on this earth. God will bless us just as soon as we are ready to receive his blessing. Reading Isaiah affirms to us that

God is a loving parent who watches over and cares for each of his children.

God has even provided a ladder upon which we may climb to heaven. We do so by becoming more and more like him, over time acquiring his divine attributes. God arranges our lives and circumstances so that we can grow and accomplish this divine destiny. Our course will be as individual as our different personalities, but our joy with God will be the same. The ancient prophet Isaiah saw that these things could be so. Because he saw the end from the beginning, Isaiah serves as a sure guide for us today.

# Chapter 1

# Visions of the End of the World

No one really knows how the Hebrew prophets experienced what they saw and heard. The prophets themselves didn't always know whether they were in their physical bodies when they had their visions. What they saw seemed to occur before their eyes as if it were happening right then. Yet, these visionaries—called "seers" in the Bible—claimed to see and hear events still in the future. And what they saw of the future was consistent with what Hebrew prophets before them had seen and heard.

For example, Daniel saw several symbolic visions of the end of the world. Whenever Daniel had a vision, he was perplexed, because what he saw affected him personally, as if he himself were involved with the events. An angel—whom Daniel describes as a "man"—told him repeatedly that what he had seen would occur at the end of the world, not in his day. After Daniel wrote down his visions, an angel instructed him to seal up the scroll and go his way. The angel told him that the visions and their interpretation would be kept from people's understandings until the end of the world.

Here's another example. John, on the island of Patmos, had a vision in which he saw and heard events in the "Lord's day" or the "day of the Lord." In the writings of the Hebrew prophets, the "day of the Lord" is a great future day of judgment, not the Sabbath. In that future day, the God of Israel will remove wicked people from the earth and deliver from calamity those who repent. John, in other words, was not just seeing things on a Sunday, as some have supposed. He was somehow actually present in a day still future, seeing and hearing the same kinds of things that former prophets had seen.

## The Pattern of Hebrew Prophecy

Bible commentators call prophetic writings that deal with the end of the world "apocalyptic" prophecy. Those that are not specific about the end of the world they call "classical" prophecy. Generally, these are considered two distinctly different literatures. The first concerns itself with events to take place in the "last days," while the second predicts events to happen in the prophets' own day.

Yet, all prophetic writings, whether about the end of the world or not, share common visionary elements. The apocalyptic imagery John uses, describing what he sees and hears, has its roots in the prior classical prophecies of Isaiah, Jeremiah, Ezekiel, Zechariah, and others. The harlot Babylon, the dragon, the beast, the woman fleeing into the wilderness, the Lamb, the servants of God on Mount Zion—all of which John speaks—first appear in prophetic writings before his time. So, while the visions of Daniel and John were entirely their own, one cannot isolate them from those of other prophets.

Indeed, all such visions build upon and complement each other. Each seems to provide a piece of a picture that is bigger than itself, that makes most sense as part of a larger whole. In whatever period of Israel's history a prophet prophesied, and whether their visions refer to the endtime or not, a common thread links them all.

The common thread of prophetic visions become clearer when we temporarily lay aside the details of a prophecy and look at its overall *pattern*. If we were to put all prophetic visions side by side, we would notice that their common elements form a picture of their own. In other words, the core ideas of these prophecies, looked at all together, compose a kind of proto-vision, a blueprint of individual visions.

Let's look at some examples. Consider the *pattern* of the classical Hebrew prophets, from Isaiah to

Malachi. Notice the ideas they have in common. Each prophet speaks of the wickedness of God's people and of the nations of the world. Each prophet warns them to repent of their abominations. If they do not, God will punish them for their sins. In the "day of the Lord," he will raise up a cruel and militaristic world power from the North that will invade and destroy their lands. Many will be killed by burning and by war, while others will be captured and taken away as slaves. These things constitute the *negative* or judgment aspects of classical prophecy.

In his mercy, however, God will spare the righteous in that day. He will provide deliverance for those who serve him and will restore them to lands of inheritance. God will raise up a deliverer who will defend their cause. God will overthrow the oppressive evil power when that power's work of retribution is done. Those who trust in God, their Maker, will survive destruction and inherit even greater blessings than before. Then follows a wonderful period of universal peace, after the wicked have been cleansed from the earth. These things constitute the *positive* or restoration aspects of classical prophecy.

### The Prophetic Pattern in Israel's History

Let's briefly examine this *pattern* of prophecy as it develops from prophet to prophet. In Isaiah's day (circa 742–700 B.C.), God's people consisted of two divided kingdoms. The tribe of Ephraim dominated the Northern Kingdom of Israel and the tribe of Judah headed up the Southern Kingdom.

According to the pattern we've been discussing, the militaristic superpower from the North that Isaiah describes was Assyria. Assyria destroyed and took captive the Northern Kingdom in Isaiah's lifetime. These events fulfilled the *negative* aspects of Isaiah's prophecy. Some of their *positive* aspects were also fulfilled during Isaiah's lifetime—in the days of Hezekiah, king of Judah—and later, in the days of Cyrus, king of Persia. But Isaiah's predictions of Israel's restoration don't match exactly those ancient happenings, because Isaiah tailored the telling of the story to fit another time frame—the end of the world.

A hundred years after Isaiah, in Jeremiah's day (circa 627–598 B.C.), the people of God consisted of the Southern Kingdom of Judah. The militaristic superpower from the North was Babylon, which repeated Assyria's scenario of destruction and captivity. The Babylonians destroyed Judah and desolated the temple in Jerusalem. These things fulfilled the *negative* aspects of Jeremiah's prophecy.

But Jeremiah's *positive* predictions—of Israel's restoration—were again only partly fulfilled in that time period. A mere remnant of Jews returned from Babylon in the days of Ezra and Nehemiah, which scarcely fulfilled Jeremiah's predictions of a return.

Neither Jeremiah nor any other Hebrew prophet limited himself to a return of only the Jews. Without exception, prophecies of a return from exile involved all the tribes of Israel, not just Judah. In addition, such prophecies predicted Israel's return at the end of the world, not before.

Isaiah and Jeremiah set the pattern for other classical prophets. Hosea, Joel, Micah, Ezekiel, and others prophesied the same negative things—which were fulfilled in their own day—and also positive things, to be fulfilled in the "last days." If many of the positive aspects of classical prophecy, therefore, were not to be fulfilled until the end of the world, then what of their negative aspects? Could these, too, perhaps apply to the endtime? Could their negative aspects have a double fulfillment, one in the time of the prophets, the other in the endtime?

The core ideas of apocalyptic prophecy—prophecy about the end of the world—in fact, form essentially the same pattern as those of classical prophecy: the people of God (and other nations) who do not repent of wickedness will suffer destruction and dispossession at the hands of a militaristic world power from the North; those who repent, on the other hand, will experience deliverance and live on into a millennial time of peace. Further details appear as we examine each prophet's vision individually.

We could thus superimpose classical and apocalyptic prophecy one upon the other without adding or taking away an essential element of either one. Both predict negative and positive things—destruction and deliverance. Their main difference is that apocalyptic prophecy claims to be *solely* of the end-time. Classical prophecy does not. Only the positive features of classical prophecy, being of a millennial nature, are predicted for the end of the world.

Now let's look at the classical prophets Zechariah and Malachi. They lived *after* the invasions of Assyria and Babylon, and *after* the Jews returned from Babylon (circa 520–445 B.C.). Both of them, however, predict a yet future "day of the Lord": in that day, the God of Israel will destroy the wicked and deliver the righteous, with a millennial peace to follow. These predictions, then, are similar to what apocalyptic prophets prophesy about the end of the world. They are also similar to what Isaiah, Jeremiah, and other classical prophets predicted *before* Israel's judgment and exile. Though far separated by events in time, the prophetic pattern of all these prophets is the same. They predict both destruction and deliverance, even though in Zachariah's and Malachi's day the time of judgment was supposedly past.

Paradoxically, most scholars say that Isaiah's prophecies of a "day of the Lord" were fulfilled by Assyria and that Jeremiah's prophecies of a "day of the Lord" were fulfilled by Babylon. If that is so, then what about Zechariah's and Malachi's prophecies of a still-future "day of the Lord"? Are there many "days of the Lord" or just one?

The *pattern* of prophecy—the core ideas all Hebrew prophecies have in common—tells us there is only one "day of the Lord" that fulfills all prophecy. That "day of the Lord," a day still future, has some precedents in ancient times. The great future "day of the Lord" *will be like* the times of destruction and deliverance in the days of Isaiah, Jeremiah, and others. That one "day of the Lord" alone, however, will fulfill all prophetic expectations, negative and positive.

## Ancient Names as Codenames

The supposition that the classical prophets knew that their predictions could have a double fulfillment—one in their own day, another in the endtime—becomes clearer when we solve an important paradox of Hebrew prophecy: prophets, both classical and apocalyptic, deal with future events in terms of nations and peoples already familiar to them. Most of the time, such nations are contemporary with the prophet. Or, such nations may have existed before the prophet's lifetime, but no longer may be the force they once were.

Isaiah characterizes Assyria and Egypt as two world powers of his day—two superpowers. In a military confrontation, he predicts, Assyria—the world power from the North—will ravage and subjugate Egypt. The fact that Isaiah's prediction was fulfilled in his own day, however, doesn't preclude the possibility that his prophecy will have a second fulfillment at the end of the world. Daniel, for example, sees a great war that involves the kingdoms of Persia and Greece, both world powers in his day. Yet, Daniel's vision is about the end of the world, not about his own day. John, on the other hand, sees a vision of an endtime "Babylon." That Babylon resembles the old Babylonian empire, which existed long before John's time. But what John sees is clearly a new Babylon, not the old.

Names of particular nations, therefore, may not help us much to understand a prophetic vision, especially a vision of the endtime. In fact, the nations the prophets mention may no longer exist. While there may be a modern Persia, Greece, or Egypt, such nations resemble the old only in name, location, and possibly ethnic identity. Today, they are political powers that are relatively insignificant compared to those the prophets saw in their visions. The prophets' visions of the future reflect such nations' ancient roles as major world powers, not the roles—if any—of their modern namesakes. If we try to identify modern Egypt with ancient Egypt or modern Iraq with ancient Babylon, for example, we are bound to get confused. We need to find another way to interpret these names of nations.

A more fruitful way to interpret their names is to examine the prophetic *pattern*. If the identity of the militaristic world power from the North in classical prophecy changes from prophet to prophet, while its role remains the same, then what does the name matter? The name doesn't matter so much as the *role* the world power fulfills; and its role is the same in both classical and apocalyptic prophecy. In the prophetic pattern, the *role*, not the name, is a constant. Could the prophets thus all be speaking of one and the same world power, so far as an endtime scenario is concerned? The name of this world power in any given instance in Israel's history would simply be a symbol or codename for an endtime world power, whose role, not whose name, is the important thing.

If that were the case—if the names of ancient world powers are codenames for endtime superpowers—then the militaristic "king of the North" in the apocalyptic Book of Daniel would be the same as the militaristic king of Assyria, also from the North, in the classical prophecy of Isaiah. Then, Isaiah's prophecies about the "king of Assyria" and Jeremiah's prophecies about the "king of Babylon" could suddenly become relevant to another time and place— to the end of the world—besides being relevant to their own day. The information these prophets give could then be used to create a more accurate picture of events still to come, perhaps in our day. In effect, just as the future "day of the Lord" *will be like* the ancient days of destruction and deliverance, so the superpowers in that day *will be like* their ancient counterparts.

## Types for a Future Worldwide Judgment

In summing up, the case made by the *pattern* of Hebrew prophecy, whether classical or apocalyptic, is that at the end of the world there will take place a twofold scenario. There will occur a worldwide judgment and destruction resembling ancient scenarios of judgment and destruction, because of the wickedness of people. At the same time, there will occur a restoration of God's people, such as was partly fulfilled anciently, in which God will deliver the righteous.

The classical prophets, like their apocalyptic counterparts, did see marvelous visions. They didn't speak of an endtime deliverance and restoration of God's people as an isolated idea. When God delivered his people from bondage in Egypt, their deliverance wasn't complete until Pharaoh's armies were destroyed. Their restoration as heirs of Abraham, Isaac, and Jacob wasn't complete until they had inherited the promised land.

Just so, deliverance for God's people at the end of the world will mean deliverance from a catastrophic destruction. God will release his people from the awful oppression of evil world powers, as in the visions of Daniel and John. The wicked will be destroyed in that day so that tyranny will finally cease. God will restore his people to perpetual lands of inheritance, where they will enjoy everlasting peace.

Both apocalyptic and classical prophecy supply the necessary information about this twofold scenario. The former does so by means of direct prophecy–by actually predicting the end of the world. The latter predicts essentially the same things but mostly by another means–by supplying historical precedents or types.

The Hebrew prophets themselves recognized this typological dimension of Israel's history. They built it into their prophecies. The prophet Zechariah, for example, talks about "Assyria" and "Egypt" as world powers that God will put down in the great future day of destruction and deliverance. But Assyria and Egypt were not even a threat to Israel at the time Zechariah was prophesying. In Zechariah's day, these nations were no longer a force to be reckoned with. This is a good example of how a prophet speaks of the rise and fall of two future superpowers that *will be like* ancient Assyria and Egypt. He simply uses the names "Assyria" and "Egypt" as codenames.

This typological use of names demands that we go back in time and look at how such nations related to Israel in their heyday—when they wielded their greatest influence. Assyria and Egypt were at a peak of their power in relation to Israel in Isaiah's day, several hundred years before Zechariah. Because all Hebrew prophecy builds upon itself, we may best understand Zechariah's prophecy about "Assyria" and "Egypt" in the light of what former prophets like Isaiah had to say about them.

Isaiah describes Assyria as being from the North, oppressive and ruthless, a law unto itself, militaristic, and intent on ruling the world. Assyria enslaved other nations, took over their lands, and inspired fear in people's hearts. When God's people and other nations had ripened in wickedness, Assyria briefly appeared to make peace. Then, suddenly—in the "day of the Lord"—Assyria burst forth like a flood and swept through the earth. According to Isaiah, Assyria conquered and destroyed all nations.

In contrast, Egypt was an elite, civilized nation. Isaiah characterizes Egypt as industrious, but suffering economic woes; politically stable, but fast deteriorating; religious, but turning to idolatry; having fertile lands, but experiencing adverse weather. The smaller nations of the world looked to Egypt's vast forces of chariots and horsemen for protection against Assyria. Egypt was the only power sufficiently strong to counter Assyria. God chastised his people for looking to Egypt for help against Assyria.

That sort of trust was relying on an arm of flesh. God required his people to look to him and trust in him to deliver them.

We may thus anticipate a similar scenario at the end of the world in a final fulfillment of Isaiah's and Zechariah's prophecies. In conjunction with that scenario, however, we may also anticipate the millennial peace that these prophets predict for God's people. The earth will attain a paradisiacal state, the lamb and the lion will lie down together, and a glorious peace will cover the earth—after it is cleansed of wickedness.

Thus, when we apply classical prophecy in general to the end of the world—just as we do apocalyptic prophecy—certain paradoxical problems disappear: prophecies that seemed to fail or were only partly fulfilled become prophecies awaiting an endtime fulfillment; prophecies of a millennial peace do not stand alone but involve a worldwide judgment; future world powers called by ancient names describe modern superpowers fulfilling similar roles.

Hebrew prophecy, both classical and apocalyptic, informs us about the end of the world. Because classical prophecy supplies a much fuller picture of the endtime scenario than apocalyptic prophecy does, it would be unfortunate to simply relegate major parts of it to ancient history. By considering all Hebrew prophecy together, we obtain a clearer view of the "last days," a view that becomes increasingly important as that time draws nearer.

# Chapter 2

# Messages Concealed
in Form and Structure

Like all good literature, Hebrew prophecy is not one-dimensional. It consists of more than just predictions about the future. The writings of many Hebrew prophets are carefully structured works of art. In no instance is this more apparent than in the Book of Isaiah. In his writings, Isaiah has captured the past and the future, the earthly and the heavenly, prophecy and theology all in one.

Perhaps surprisingly, a literature that compares with Isaiah in many respects are fairy tales. This is not to say that Isaiah's writings, like fairy tales, are ficticious; far from it. Fairy tales resemble the prophecies of Isaiah in the sense that they deal with archetypes of good and evil. The wicked ogre or giant, who tries to kill the hero but ends up dead himself, corresponds with the king of Assyria/Babylon, who seeks to annihilate the people of God. The cruel, despotic stepmother corresponds with the harlot Babylon. She subjugates and oppresses the virgin Zion or the righteous people of God. Fairy godmothers correspond to angels or messengers whom God empowers, by whose means God intervenes in the affairs of his people in times of crisis.

Fairy tales concern themselves in particular with a hero or heroine who must go through a series of ordeals in order to "live happily ever after." On one level they speak to us of our own happiness, projecting what obstacles we all must overcome in order to achieve that goal. At the same time, they describe the actual journey, obstacles, and outcome for a specific hero or heroine. This double level of meaning is also found in Isaiah.

Both Isaiah and fairy tales reveal that true happiness—eternal life and exaltation—comes only after a period of severe trial and humiliation during which the hero and heroine nearly perish. Indeed, a hero and a heroine attain this other-worldly state of happiness only when they follow, to the letter, the higher wisdom that is offered them. (Those given the same opportunity, who refuse to submit to wisdom and trials, end up as ugly stepsisters and other villainous characters in the story.) Perhaps that is why it is never made clear whether the castle in which the prince and princess live happily ever after is on earth or in heaven. Their true home is earthly and heavenly at the same time.

### Structure and Content—Two Dimensions

Such commonalities in fairy tales and the Book of Isaiah give an idea of the literary nature of Isaiah's prophecy. The book's literary features, however, are particularly apparent in the way the book is organized—in the structures or literary forms Isaiah uses to convey his thought.

The structure of a book determines the order and manner in which a writer presents his material. What ideas should come first? Who will be the cast of characters and how should he develop them? Will there be a climactic unfolding of ideas, a happy ending, etc.? Yet, a structure doesn't determine actual words or content. Rather, it dictates how the content will be introduced. When God commissions Isaiah as a prophet, he inspires Isaiah what to say. But how Isaiah says it may be an individual thing. As you read the Bible, you can't help but notice the different literary styles and methods the Hebrew prophets use. Their messages or content may be similar. But the way they present them reflects their individual personalities and literary skill.

An important idea, central to helping you understand Isaiah, is that the structure of the book conveys its own message, a message in addition to the actual content. Just as we use a different form for a letter than for a poem, a short story, or a contract, so the different ways in which the prophet organizes his material tells us something about his intent. A structure that progressively builds one idea upon another is different from a simple sequence or chain of ideas. A structure that repeatedly alternates themes, like *chaos* and *creation,* differs from a series of themes that are linked together domino fashion.

Understanding the structures of the Book of Isaiah, in fact, is as important as understanding the individual words; they are two distinct dimensions of the same prophecy. Drawing on the old adage, we are sometimes on more familiar ground among the trees, dealing with specific verses from Isaiah to support our thoughts or beliefs. Still, the broader view of the forest with its contours, expanse, and diversity reveals much more.

## Trouble at Home, Exile Abroad, Happy Homecoming

Just as an American writer today may use the literary techniques of other cultures to enrich his style, so Isaiah enhances his writings by using literary patterns or structures from other Near Eastern cultures.

His message, of course, is purely Hebrew. The Hebrews were always unique in their beliefs and worldview. Isaiah adapts other nations' literary patterns for his own purpose, for a divine purpose.

Let's look at an example, an Egyptian structure Isaiah utilizes to convey a prophetic message. The Egyptians, many centuries before Isaiah, wove narrative stories around three themes—trouble at home, exile abroad, and happy homecoming. The story of Sinuhe provides a classic example. Sinuhe, who belongs to the royal family of Egypt, finds himself involved in a political intrigue. He is forced to flee his country to save his life. Away from home, among a foreign people and culture, Sinuhe gains experience and self-awareness. Years of exile mature him. As he comes to understand himself, who he is, he is filled with an overwhelming desire to return home. Meanwhile, the political climate in his homeland has changed. His life is no longer in danger. On the contrary, he is escorted home in honor and with great fanfare. Sinuhe is appointed to a high position.

That is also the story of Israel. Isaiah frames his entire book around this three-part pattern. The people of Israel, too, find themselves in trouble in their homeland (Isaiah 1–39). Because of wickedness, God exiles them into the world at large (Isaiah 40–54). There, they interact with peoples and gain experience and self-awareness. As they realize their true identity—who they are—they repent of their sins and renew their allegiance to God. At that point, they are escorted home in a glorious and happy homecoming (Isaiah 55–66). God appoints them as priests and royal ministers to the remainder of his peoples. A millennial peace begins.

## A Distinction between Prophecy and History

This structure of trouble at home, exile abroad, and happy homecoming has caused a lot of controversy among scholars. They have not recognized the book's three successive parts as a literary structure. Instead, many scholars have used these three parts to advance the theory that the Book of Isaiah was written by three different authors. They have assumed that its three distinct settings—Israel before, during, and after the exile—originated in three different time periods of Israel's history. They have also assumed that the third of the three settings—Israel's return from exile—coincided with the Jews' return from Babylon.

Such assumptions, however, imply that Isaiah was not a prophet but a historian. Isaiah prophesied the return of all the tribes of Israel, not just the Jews. He predicted they would come home from the four directions of the earth, not just Babylon. Many Jews never returned from exile, nor did the whole body of the ten northern tribes. Isaiah's prophecy, scholars contend, must therefore have failed.

It is not Isaiah's prophecy that has failed, however, but scholars who have failed to discern the literary structure of the Book of Isaiah, refusing to take Isaiah at his word. By means of literary devices, Isaiah reveals that Israel will return from exile at the end of the world, not before.

Many scholars also imply that Isaiah could not have seen the future to know what would happen to Israel. How could a person possibly describe Israel's future exile and beyond as if he had actually been there? There seemed to be no precedent for such a thing, at least not before Isaiah's time. So scholars said there had to be another explanation—three authors.

From a literary standpoint, however, it makes perfect sense to depict Israel in three different settings. Prophets prophesy; they don't just chronicle current events. If he was a visionary who saw the future, then he would describe it as if he had actually seen it. Far from providing grounds for multiple authors, this structure argues for one—a single author who comprehended the whole scope of Israel's history, who saw the end from the beginning. Isaiah's threefold pattern tells us that Israel's history doesn't end when she goes into exile. It resumes when Israel returns home—all part of a divine plan.*

---

*Coinciding with Isaiah's three-part structure appears an emphasis on nationalism, universalism, and individualism. A national Israel fails to repent and is scattered among the nations

In Hebrew literature, a nation may undergo in its history what its ancestor or king undergoes in his life. In that sense, the ancestor or king personifies his people. Several ancestors of God's people provide a precedent for Isaiah's literary structure. For example, Jacob, father of the nation Israel, experienced this threefold cycle in his life. When his twin brother Esau seeks to kill him, Jacob flees into the land of Haran. There he interacts with people, marries, and has children. He acquires flocks and herds and attains considerable stature. At that point, God summons him back to the promised land. On his return, he dwells in strength as one of Israel's patriarchs.

## Apostasy, Judgment, Restoration, Salvation

A second cycle of themes around which Isaiah structures his book consists of apostasy (Isaiah 1–9), judgment (Isaiah 10–34), restoration (Isaiah 35–59), and salvation (Isaiah 60–66). He utilizes a fourfold Canaanite structure to convey these ideas. It comes from the myth of Baal and Anath, which is based on the four themes of threat, war, victory, and feast. Isaiah modifies and adapts this structure for his own

---

(Isaiah 1-39). A universal Israel awakens to her national identity—they are still the people of God (Isaiah 40–54). Individuals who repent return home from exile and resume that national identity (Isaiah 55–66).

prophetic purpose. He keeps the Canaanite structure but changes the essence to themes that are peculiarly Hebrew.

In this structure, Isaiah shows how Israel, by choosing to sin, has never been in a worse condition. God's people have become alienated from their Maker; they have become like other nations. God commissions the king of Assyria against them and punishes them for their crimes by letting other nations rule them. But the time will come when he will restore his people, teach them his law, and send his word among them. He will plead with them to repent and return to him. As they respond to his love, God himself comes and reestablishes peace among them.

Many details in the Book of Isaiah fill out this fourfold succession of themes, which also appears in individual passages. These four themes again point to a glorious future for Israel. Israel may have broken the covenant she made with her God and punishment may have followed. But when she repents of wickedness God will restore her to lands of inheritance and a long-awaited peace will commence.

As we comprehend this structure, we again see how Israel's history follows a predetermined plan. It doesn't end with Israel's destruction in the era of the prophets, but it will resume in a future time of restoration.

## Threat One, Threat Two, Threat Three

A third structure Isaiah adapts consists of a literary pattern common to Babylonian writing, which uses threat one (Isaiah 1–38), threat two (Isaiah 39–48), and threat three (Isaiah 49–66). In the Book of Isaiah, these threats become three tests God's people must pass in order to inherit a millennial peace. Such tests have a refining effect on Israel. When Israel passes the tests, she demonstrates her loyalty to God. At the same time, the tests weed out from God's people those who will not repent.

The king of Assyria/Babylon, in the first part of the book, poses threat one: will Israel give her allegiance to him or to her God? If she gives her allegiance to the king of Assyria/Babylon, she will enjoy temporary benefits but suffer an everlasting loss. If she gives her allegiance to God, there will be temporary challenges but God will deliver her and espouse her forever.

Idolaters and the goods they sell, in the second part of the book, pose threat two: will Israel worship things made by human hands, or will she worship God, her Maker? If she worships idols, she will find that focusing on material pleasures brings spiritual blindness. She may, in the end, come away empty-handed. But if she worships God, he promises to bless her now and always. She has only to put that to the test.

False brethren, in the third part of the book, create threat three: will Israel yield to pressure from evil authorities or will she trust in God and wait for his deliverance? She can join religious and civil authorities among her people in persecuting those who follow righteousness, and then she herself will not come under attack. But by taking that course, she will ultimately be cut off from God's people. On the other hand, if she joins herself to God and suffers persecution because she bears his name, then God will ultimately deliver her from shame. He will exalt her as his spouse in the sight of all peoples.

## The Curses and the Blessings

A fourth structure parallels the covenants that Hittite emperors made with vassal kings and their peoples. Ancient covenant documents from the Near East have been found that stipulate the terms of these covenants. They mention certain blessings and curses that would follow a vassal king's faithfulness or unfaithfulness to the covenant. If the vassal king kept the terms of the covenant, blessings or good fortune would result. If the vassal did not keep the terms of the covenant, he and his people would suffer curses or misfortunes.

So it was in God's covenant with Israel. Israel's faithfulness or unfaithfulness to the covenant would bring blessings or curses. Moses outlined these blessings and curses for Israel so she would know the consequences of her actions (see Deuteronomy 28). By her own choosing, Israel would be blessed or cursed by God.

In the first half of the Book of Isaiah (Isaiah 1–39), Israel suffers the curses of the covenant. Israel and her kings have broken their covenants with God. Every misfortune that the covenants mention is coming upon her. In the second half of the book (Isaiah 40–66), blessings prevail. God renews the covenant with his people and they renew their allegiance to him. They again enjoy God's blessings. Isaiah has structured his book to reflect these two main covenant ideas.

Exceptions to this overall pattern nonetheless occur. Some blessings appear among the curses and some curses appear among the blessings. These exceptions suggest that not all Israel needs to suffer the curses of the covenant. Even in a time of national wickedness and calamity, God will deliver the righteous. On the other hand, not everyone will enjoy God's glorious promises. Only those who keep the terms of the covenant qualify for God's blessings.

The Hittite structure that Isaiah uses reverses the structure of the covenant God made with Israel. In God's covenant with Israel, Moses stipulated first the blessings, then the curses. That is the opposite of what Isaiah does. By Isaiah's time, however, Israel's circumstances had changed. The Northern Kingdom had already proven unfaithful to the covenant and was suffering the consequences. At some point, according to Isaiah, God will act to bring Israel back to a state of blessedness. Israel's future holds the promise of God's restored blessings.

## Destruction of the Wicked/ Deliverance of the Righteous

A fifth structure is formed by linking three ideas: destruction of the wicked (Isaiah 1–39), deliverance of the righteous (Isaiah 40–66), at the presence of a righteous king, a descendant of King David (Isaiah 36–38). This structure, like the others, encompasses the entire book, which is organized in three parts to reflect these three ideas. This structure occurs in many individual passages as well. Almost anywhere in the book that the name *Zion* appears, these three ideas are linked together.

By looking for this linking of ideas we can better comprehend what Isaiah would say about Zion. The most important idea is that Zion or Jerusalem is a safe place. Isaiah weaves a whole ideology or set of principles around that concept—a Zion ideology. The place Zion or Jerusalem is made safe by virtue of the righteousness of its king, who is a loyal vassal (or servant) of God. If ever there's a threat to the people, the king may appeal to God for help. God will deliver both the king and his people so long as the king proves faithful to the terms of God's covenant and, in turn, the people prove themselves loyal to their king. God made this covenant with King David and his heirs, and so it is called the Davidic covenant.

Whenever the three ideas mentioned earlier appear together, a situation occurs where faithfulness to God's covenant is put to the test: God's people are threatened by an opposing power; their king, a legitimate heir of King David, appeals to God for help; God destroys their enemies and delivers his people. The people's safety actually lies in God's response to the king's intercession on their behalf.

This threefold structure may have originated with the Jebusites, who inhabited Zion or Jerusalem before the Israelites. The Jebusites appear to have descended from Melchizedek, who was a righteous king and priest of that city. Like Melchizedek, whose name means "king of righteousness," Jebusite kings included the word "righteous" or "righteousness" in their names. The Jebusites in David's time were overly confident of their safety before David captured the city for Israel.

In the time of Isaiah and Hezekiah, such confidence was justified. Hezekiah, king of Judah, was a righteous descendant of King David. In his day, an Assyrian army of 185,000 men surrounded Zion or Jerusalem and demanded its surrender (see Isaiah 36).

Because Hezekiah was loyal to God, and because the people were loyal to Hezekiah, God heard the king's appeal for help (see Isaiah 37–38). An angel of God struck the Assyrian horde with a plague, so that in one night all died. Thus God delivered his people.

## Isaiah's Structures Reveal a Divine Plan

As you consider these and other structures in the Book of Isaiah, I hope you will begin to see what remarkable literary skill Isaiah was using. Isaiah not only adapts a variety of Near Eastern patterns in organizing his material, he layers them one upon another. He forms his entire book around them; much of the book's content was developed to accommodate them.

The more one analyzes these structures, the more the idea of three authors in different time periods appears unreasonable. Here is a vision, presented from different angles, that transcends all time. Its sublime and sweeping range spans all history. It puts in perspective all human experience. Why limit one's focus to individual parts of that vision?

Each of Isaiah's structures conceals and reveals a message, a divine message. That message comprehends the past and the future in one. It doesn't reflect the hopeful optimism of a mere mortal, but instead reveals the all-encompassing plan of a loving God. We thus see that God's plan ever seeks to provide for and redeem his children. Isaiah's structures testify that God is at the helm of his children's destiny. They affirm not only that God ordained the end from the beginning, but that Israel's golden age is yet to come.

# Chapter 3

# The Recycling of History

As Isaiah informs us, God "foretell[s] the end from the beginning" (Isaiah 46:10). That may seem an obvious statement, coming from a prophet. But we already know it doesn't just mean that God predicts the future in plain words. God's revelation is multi-dimensional. He also foretells the end by orchestrating history itself so that what happened in the beginning will happen again in the end. The end is thus foretold—from the beginning—in Israel's very history. Israel's future (and the world's) is contained in her past.

Understanding this concept—that events in Israel's history will repeat themselves—is essential to understanding the prophecy of Isaiah. Everything, in fact, that Isaiah predicts for the future has a precedent, or counterpart, in the past. He prophesies nothing really new. His entire vision of the future consists of new versions of events that took place in ancient times.

This orchestration of human history according to a predetermined plan, Isaiah proclaims, proves that God is real, that he is divine. Only God can foreordain history in this manner. That he will do in the future what he has done before, moreover, is a comfort to those who will experience the end. It serves as a guide to God's people in troubled times, a help in identifying what is real amidst confusion.

## The Past Foreshadows the Future

If we can learn about Israel's past, therefore, we can learn firsthand what will occur in her future. Maybe that's why God commands Israel to celebrate the Passover each year. When people relive the story of the exodus out of Egypt, the wandering in the wilderness, and the inheritance of the promised land, they are being prepared for these events to happen again.

However, Isaiah does not say that everything will happen in exactly the way it once did. Instead, Isaiah selects those parts of past events, and of events out of his own time, that he knows are going to occur again. Isaiah is not alone in this technique; other prophets do the same. Jeremiah and Ezekiel, for example, prophesy a new exodus of God's people out of all the countries where God has scattered them. Jeremiah predicts that the new exodus will so

44

surpass the old that the old will no longer be celebrated. Ezekiel and Hosea prophesy a new wandering in the wilderness resembling the former. Jeremiah says that these events as well as Israel's reinheritance of the promised land will occur at the end of the world.

Isaiah does not outline an explicit step-by-step sequence of new events patterned after the old. Rather, he creates an implicit sequence or chronology throughout his book. He builds this sequence by linking events domino fashion—by prophesying the same event several times in different combinations with other events. These combinations create links between events that at first may appear unrelated.

Take the new exodus for example. In one part of his book, Isaiah predicts a new exodus of God's people out of Babylon, accompanied by God's presence. In another part of his book, he associates a new wandering in the wilderness with the new exodus out of Babylon. In another, he identifies "Babylon" as the world's wicked inhabitants, whom the king of Assyria destroys in the "day of the Lord." In another part, Isaiah predicts that God's people will return from throughout the earth at the very time of the worldwide destruction. Elsewhere, he describes the exodus of God's people from the four directions of the earth to Zion. In yet another place, Isaiah describes God's people streaming out of all nations to Zion. Again, he identifies Zion as a place where God's cloud of glory covers and protects God's people. Finally, he identifies people of all nations streaming to Zion in the "last days"—at the end of the world—giving us a time frame. In Zion, God's people receive inheritances of land. And so forth.

In this manner, Isaiah interconnects all new versions of old events to one another. This linking and correlating of events throughout the book is itself one of Isaiah's literary structures. But because the book's chronology is not obvious, some have speculated that Isaiah is a haphazard assemblage of things in the past. It's true that we are often dealing with parts and pieces from different portions of Israel's past placed together in seemingly disconnected passages. However, Isaiah has actually crafted these pieces into a brand-new prophecy. That prophecy displays amazing internal consistency from beginning to end; it evidences obvious foresight and skill. It links together all parts of the book, outlining in detail a momentous time to come.

The idea of linking many events into a single sequence—within a time frame that is still future—takes a little getting used to. But by piecing them together from different parts of the book, we can put together an approximate chronology.

## A Future Chronology of Past Events

Isaiah's chronology of new events varies in several ways from what took place anciently. For one thing, the order in which the events occur may not be the same. Another difference is that the former events happened over several millennia, but the new events will happen within a very brief time span. By linking the whole "domino" sequence of events to the "last days," Isaiah lets us know that they will occur at the end of the world. Similarly, by identifying many of these same events as taking place in the "day of the Lord," Isaiah establishes the "day of the Lord" in the endtime.

One of the first things to occur in Isaiah's endtime sequence is Israel's apostasy or rebellion. As we read about that event, we need to understand just exactly whom he's talking about. It helps to bear in mind that God scattered Israel to the ends of the earth—among all nations. The Jews who retained their identity as part of Israel were only a minority among many Israelites whom God scattered. Many other Jews lost their identity as Jews, as they were assimilated into the Gentiles. In addition, the ten northern tribes of Israel became lost from history when the Assyrians took them captive. But none is lost to a loving God who says, through the prophets, that he will remember his people.*

---

*Interestingly, one of the articles of belief of Judaism today concerns the return and restoration of the Ten Tribes of Israel. Over the centuries, the Jews have made many efforts to discover and reclaim their non-Jewish kinsmen. They still look forward to the prophesied reunion of Judah and Ephraim. The Jews also believe that certain "righteous Gentiles" will be part of future Israel, including Gentiles who, in reality, are assimilated Israelites.

Isaiah's prophecies thus address two kinds of Israelites throughout the world: those like the Jews, who have been able to maintain their ethnic integrity; and those who were assimilated among the nations, who have become identified as Gentiles. We might refer to these as "ethnic" Israel, on the one hand, and "assimilated" Israel, on the other.

When Isaiah speaks of Israel's apostasy and rebellion, therefore, he is speaking of those who become alienated from God—who break their covenant with the God of Israel—at the end of the world. We see this alienation expressed in the marriage imagery the prophets frequently employ to describe Israel's relationship to her God. When Israel breaks her covenant, God casts her off, but not forever. He seeks to reclaim her as soon as she ceases her adulteries and returns to him.

Isaiah adapts this marriage imagery into the idea of two women. One symbolizes those who are "ethnic" Israel, who were cast off in the past, but whom God now reclaims. The other symbolizes those who are "assimilated" Israel, whom God has espoused, but who now turn adulterous, unrepentant. Both women have known the God of Israel as their husband. The first represents those who rejected God anciently, whom he now receives back. The second represents those who have been the people of God, who now reject him.

The latter group, not the former, is the subject of Israel's apostasy in the Book of Isaiah. It's important to make a distinction between the two or we could impute apostasy to the wrong group of people. While both peoples of God exist throughout the world, only one rebels.

In Isaiah's prophecy, two main sins cause Israel's apostasy: injustice and idolatry. The poor among God's people are oppressed and many suffer want. The entire society seems on the point of breaking down. Isaiah denounces the people's political leaders as irresponsible and guilty of gross crimes. They have become as the leaders of Sodom and as the people of Gomorrah. They shamelessly and openly commit adultery. Rapine, bribery, and murder have become prevalent. The people's religious leaders flatter them and feed them falsehoods. Money and the things money buys have become people's gods.

These false gods cannot save the people in the day of judgment. All who remain in Babylon and cling to their idols will be destroyed as was Babylon of old. According to Isaiah, God will destroy the wicked and erase sinners from the face of the earth just as he destroyed the people of Sodom and Gomorrah.

## Doomsday for the Wicked

From how I have pieced together Isaiah's chronology, the following series of events appears to describe the end of the world. As a result of the apostasy of God's people, calamity will overtake the world, as at the time of the Flood. It will come as a flood from the North. God will cleanse the earth by fire and by the sword, and few of its inhabitants will survive. The king of Assyria/Babylon will shake and terrify the nations. He will seek to annihilate and exterminate entire nations. He will feign peace and deceive the nations, then treacherously and unexpectedly attack them. Like an inundating deluge of mighty waters, his armies will invade all countries. They will serve as the instruments of God's wrath to cause destruction throughout the earth. Like a flooding scourge, they will sweep through the land, leaving havoc and disaster in their wake. They will turn the world into a wilderness.

The king of Assyria/Babylon will tread peoples underfoot and cruelly oppress them. He will plunder their wealth and annex all lands. He will do away with the borders of nations. He will subdue all peoples and make himself ruler of the world. He will ascend above the clouds and set his throne in the heavens, thinking himself the equal of God.

The "day of the Lord" will come as a cruel outburst of anger and wrath to make the earth a desolation. There will be disturbance in the heavens; the land will flow with lava. The very earth will be jarred out of place and reel to and fro like a drunkard.

Whole cities will be turned into flying chaff and dust in an instant. They will be consumed amid thunderous quakings, tempestuous blasts, and conflagrations of devouring fire. They will billow upward in mushrooming clouds of smoke. The earth will be scorched and people themselves will be fuel for the fire. Towers will collapse and mountains will be removed.

A pall of darkness will cover the earth like sackcloth and obscure the light of the sun, moon, and stars. Incurable plagues will break out that will eradicate people like vermin. People's corpses will cover the land, lying like litter about the streets. Those still alive will flee in panic and live in utter destitution. They will hide in caves and dens, mourning because they had not repented of their sins. Chaos, anarchy, and lawlessness will rule because their whole society became corrupt.

The Assyrians will desolate and conquer the lands of God's people. They will destroy their armies, take them captive, and yoke them with heavy burdens. They will strike them with the rod and raise their staff over them as did the Egyptians. Israel will suffer bondage because she rejected her God and refused to respond to his love. At that time, the Assyrians will lay siege to Zion and demand its surrender. Then God will descend upon Mount Zion as he did upon Mount Sinai. He will wage war on the besieging Assyrian host and consume them by his fire. He will make his voice resound and they will be terror-stricken and perish.

At this point in Isaiah's sequence, the subject changes from God's unfaithful people to those of Israel who repent. Even while God's people who became rebellious are suffering calamities, those who repent and prove loyal to God experience his deliverance. The demise of the one and redemption of the other occur simultaneously. So you will see that many of the following events overlap with the ones previously mentioned. Of course, many additional connected incidents round out this endtime scenario.

**Millennial Peace for the Righteous**

Just as we read about terror, captivity, and destruction for the wicked, so an entirely different experience comes to those who repent. These respond to God's call and return from exile. As God scattered Israel in four directions, so he gathers them again, from every country. As God called Abraham to leave his kindred and people and come into the promised land, so these come from the ends of the earth. As Lot and his daughters escaped the desolation of Sodom and Gomorrah, so these come out of all nations on the eve of the nations' desolation.

The angel of destruction will pass over them, as it passed over the Israelites in Egypt. God will preserve his people even as he destroys his people's oppressors.

Israel will return to the promised land in a great exodus like the exodus out of Egypt. This time, however, Israel's path will lead through all elements that may stand in the way. God's people will walk through fire and through the sea and through rivers. They will wander in the wilderness and in deserts as of old. Mountain ranges will be their highways.

God will guide his people home and protect them from enemies. He will lead them by springs of water and provide them with bread. The heat of the sun will not oppress them nor will wild animals molest them. A cloud of glory will cover and protect them as it protected Israel from the Egyptians. The cloud will appear over them by day and will glow like a mist of fire by night. None will be able to penetrate the cloud to do them harm.

Israel's exodus will not take place in panic or in fear. It will be like Israel's festal pilgrimage to Zion anciently. Those whom God delivers will sings songs of salvation as they march homeward. They will play the flute, the drum, and stringed instruments as they wend their way to the mountain of God. They will come rejoicing to Zion at the end of the world, their sorrows and tribulations left behind. Because they were ridiculed and put to shame for being faithful to God's covenant, God will endow them with everlasting joy. Because they were robbed and oppressed and dealt with unjustly, God will award them an everlasting inheritance.

God will raise up a deliverer for his people who will lead them as Moses led Israel. Like Moses, this deliverer will free Israel from her oppressors. He will call God's people out of all countries to Zion. He will teach them God's law and establish justice and righteousness among them. His work of delivering God's people will be as the dawning of the light before the rising sun. God will anoint and empower him and facilitate his work.

God's servant will restore the tribes of Israel and assign them lands of inheritance, just as Joshua did. He will unite Judah and Ephraim, just as David did. He will restore the lands of the nations, just as Cyrus did. He will lead Israel's victories over the Assyrian hosts and will defeat them in battle just as Gideon defeated the Midianites. He and God's people will rebuild Jerusalem and its temple. They will restore and resettle the desolate cities, as did the ancient Israelites. They will spread to all parts of the earth.

God will appoint righteous judges who will rule his people with justice. God himself will reign in their midst. His loving presence among his people will be like the light of the sun. His descent on Mount Zion will signal terror to his enemies but rejoicing to his people. God will make a new covenant with his people, an unconditional covenant, as he had with Abraham, Isaac, and Jacob. He will dwell with his people in Zion, as he dwelt with Israel in the wilderness. Zion will become as the paradise of God. The earth itself and God's people will be re-created and renewed. People will live a long time, like the ancients, and enjoy a millennial peace.

## What Has Been Shall Be Again

As we see how Isaiah links together a variety of ancient happenings to create an endtime scenario, we begin to perceive the future as a mirror of the past. This structure comprehends all Israel's history, past and future, into one whole. It maps out a complete cycle of events that will occur in that future time. It defines what Isaiah means by the "day of the Lord."

In that manner, we obtain an entirely new view of Isaiah's prophecy, one that ties all its individual parts together, that accounts for much of the content of the Book of Isaiah, showing where each piece fits. No other scenario in all Hebrew prophecy appears as cohesive and coherent. How much better it works than carving Isaiah into separate segments and then trying to make sense of them! How much more meaningful this view is than confining each segment to some incident of the past!

Isaiah cautions us not to dwell on Israel's past. God will do new things, he says. "Look at them!" But God will not do something that will catch his people off guard. He will do what he has done before. He is the same yesterday, today, and forever.

Israel's past supplies a model. As the writer of Ecclesiastes says, "What has been shall be again. What has been done shall be done again. There is nothing new under the sun. Is there anything of which one can say, 'See, this is new?' It has already occurred of old, in times before us" (Ecclesiastes 1:9–10).

# Chapter 4

# The Covenant with Israel

Whether in the past or in the future, God deals with his people Israel in the same equitable manner. As God expects Israel to do, he himself always acts within the bounds of the covenants he has entered into. In fact, God does nothing at any time unless it is within covenant relationships that he has established with his people and with individuals. As God acts or intervenes in human history, such actions underscore his faithfulness to his covenants.

## Two Types of Covenants

The covenant God made with Israel in the Sinai wilderness was a conditional covenant; the privileges of that covenant had to be earned. Its blessings depended on whether Israel kept the promises she made as terms of the covenant. The Sinai covenant differed from the covenants God had made with Israel's ancestors—Abraham, Isaac, and Jacob. With them, he made unconditional covenants. God promised them blessings and privileges as a free gift. These unconditional covenants came only after Israel's ancestors had proven themselves faithful to God under all conditions. God put each ancestor to the test, and each passed the test.

The blessings of God's covenant with Abraham, Isaac, and Jacob consisted of a promised land and an enduring posterity. God gave them the land of Canaan. He also promised that their offspring would continue and increase through all generations of time and in eternity. Their descendants would become as numerous as the sands of the seashore and as the stars in the heavens. When the Egyptians enslaved Israel and began killing her children, God took steps to preserve the posterity of those with whom he had covenanted. Like a woman in travail, Israel gave birth to a son—Moses—whom God chose as His people's deliverer.

The purpose of the Sinai covenant, which God made under Moses, was to lift Israel from a lower to a higher spiritual and physical plane—to the same level as her ancestors. In the Sinai wilderness, God officially made Israel a nation. Through Moses, God brought a nation (Israel) out of another nation (Egypt) with signs and wonders. In a sense, Egypt gave birth to Israel. God created these special circumstances in order to ennoble and elevate his people. At that time, Israel became God's people and he became their God. God sought to make an example of Israel to all nations, a testimony of what God could do for all peoples.

Before the exodus out of Egypt, the people of Israel were not officially the people of God. They were simply the descendants of Abraham, Isaac, and Jacob, much as many Israelites are today. God did not deliver them out of Egypt for any merit of theirs. On their own they could claim no covenant blessings because they themselves had made no covenant. God delivered Israel out of Egypt because of his covenants with Israel's ancestors—Abraham, Isaac, and Jacob. When the people of Israel were imperiled in Egypt, God "remembered" his covenant with their ancestors and brought their descendants out.

## The Meaning of Covenant Making

You may wonder why such unusual things happened to the Israelites as they came out of Egypt and why those events are so much detailed in the scriptural account. The events surrounding Israel's coming out of Egypt set a pattern for what God would do in the future. Everything that happened between God and Israel, in fact, was determined by covenant relationships. What will occur in the future, therefore, will likewise be determined by covenant relationships.

Even though God had promised Israel's ancestors a land of inheritance, Israel could not just go and possess it. If she did, she would be like any other aggressive nation and would subject herself to grave danger. Rather, Israel had to obtain the land for herself as a covenant blessing. The covenant God made with Israel in the Sinai wilderness provided the means by which she could obtain the land.

Similarities between ancient Near Eastern covenants and God's covenant with Israel give us added insights into the nature of God's covenant. As we understand more about the covenants ancient Near Eastern emperors made with vassal kings and their peoples, we understand more about God's covenant with Israel. Ancient Near Eastern covenant documents, in fact, spell out many things that are simply taken for granted in the cultural background of the Bible.

When God made the covenant with Israel, for example, she, *as a nation,* became God's servant or vassal. It was as if God had made the covenant with a single individual, his servant or vassal, even though that "individual" was really the whole nation. All the blessings and privileges of the covenant would be hers so long as the entire nation was faithful to God. Likewise, the curses of the covenant would fall upon her if she was unfaithful. It took forty years in the Sinai wilderness for Israel *as a nation* to finally keep the terms of God's covenant.

During the exodus out of Egypt, God showed Israel what he could or would do for her if she would be faithful to him. The exodus was a demonstration of God's power. He revealed himself to Israel as an all-powerful God, one in whom she could trust because he loved her. At that time, so long as she obeyed God's word, as Moses revealed it, all went well. What God did for her in the exodus, however, was for her ancestors' sake, as mentioned.

Once he covenanted with Israel herself, God would deliver her for her own sake. The blessings of God's covenant would be hers directly. She herself would have control of her situation. In addition, Israel could then, if she chose, go forward and attain the same privileges as her ancestors. As God had made an unconditional covenant with Abraham, Isaac, and Jacob, so he could with Israel or with individuals in Israel.

The plagues God sent on the Egyptians were again for the sake of Israel's ancestors. In ancient Near Eastern covenants, those who infringe on the rights of vassal kings bring upon themselves the curses of the covenant the emperor makes with his vassals. In other words, instead of the curses of the covenant falling on a loyal vassal, they fall on those who infringe on his rights.

By enslaving Israel and killing her children, Egypt infringed on the rights of Abraham, Isaac, and Jacob. God's covenant with them provided for the continuation and increase of their posterity. That posterity, the Egyptians now endangered. Once God covenanted with Israel herself, however, God would bring curses or plagues on any nation that infringed on *her* rights. No nation would be able to stand against her so long as she kept the terms of the covenant.

## Israel Is Responsible for Herself

The advantages of the Sinai covenant were obvious, but its terms would be difficult to keep. The whole wilderness experience involved the constant weeding out of offenders. No sooner did God make a covenant with Israel than she made and worshiped a golden calf. Only Moses' intervention prevented Israel from perishing at that time on account of the curses of her covenant. Moses appealed to God's covenant with Abraham, Isaac, and Jacob that God might spare his people. Nevertheless, all the generation that had sinned eventually died in the wilderness. God had to abide by the terms of two different covenants he had now made. He was obliged to inflict curses on those who had sinned in the wilderness, yet he had to preserve the posterity of Abraham, Isaac, and Jacob.

The generation of Israel that inherited the promised land after years of wandering was faithful to God *as a nation*. Moses had schooled them in the law of the covenant so that all kept the covenant's terms. The blessings of the covenant were now theirs to enjoy. They would receive not only the land but also God's protection. Their posterity would increase and prosper in the land so long as they remained faithful to God. No external force could prevent them now from going forward and proving themselves faithful under all conditions, as Abraham, Isaac, and Jacob had done.

A brief loss of God's protection, however, portended worse things to come. That loss of protection occurred during Israel's conquest of Canaan as the Israelites drove out the idolatrous Canaanites. When one Israelite soldier unlawfully took the spoils of war, Israel's whole army suffered a setback. By his transgression, the soldier had endangered the entire people of Israel. After the people identified the offender and put him to death, God restored his protection of Israel. As that incident again showed, God's willingness to bless his people depended on their being faithful to God *as a nation*.

As you can imagine, such complete faithfulness by an entire people would be very difficult to maintain. After the passing of Moses and Joshua, Israel's condition deteriorated. Now that she possessed the promised land, Israel became careless. Instead of keeping the terms of the covenant, people did what was right in their own eyes. It was not long before the blessings of the covenant began to fail and the curses of the covenant started happening.

When the surrounding nations saw Israel's weakness, they attacked her. Up to that point, God had delivered Israel from all her enemies. Now her enemies gained power over her. In taking possession of the promised land, Israel had vanquished many nations. Now she herself was about to be vanquished. Israel's condition became desperate. Still, her people made no further effort to keep the terms of the covenant.

## The Role of the King in Israel

The elders of Israel rightly saw that Israel's condition could not continue if she was to survive. The Philistines were about to deal the death blow to Israel. So her elders asked the prophet Samuel to anoint a king who would lead them in battle as Joshua had done. Israel needed a king who could unite the fragmented tribes and organize them to overthrow their enemies. Israel's judges, who had ruled for a time, had never fully been able to accomplish this. The main concern of the elders of Israel now was to seek the people's protection.

Samuel's first response was appropriate, reminding Israel that God was her King (her emperor). If she would keep the terms of the covenant, God would protect her. God was duty bound to come to the aid of his servant (his vassal) in the event of a mortal threat. He would annihilate a common enemy so long as Israel was faithful to him. In asking for a human king, Israel had rejected her God.

But for Israel to again become completely faithful *as a nation* would at that point be virtually impossible. The people had drifted too far from God, and they were facing their enemies right now. Special circumstances would again have to occur in order for them to attain that degree of faithfulness. It had taken Moses two generations of instruction in the wilderness to raise Israel to that level. Also, Israel could no longer appeal to God's covenant with Abraham, Isaac, and Jacob, though that covenant was still in force. Israel herself had covenanted with God directly; she herself was now responsible for obtaining God's protection.

So God agreed to Israel's demands for a king and instructed Samuel to anoint Saul. In her distress, Israel again gave birth to a son—the king of Israel—who was to become his people's deliverer. Saul, however, fell into disfavor by going against God's word. So God told Samuel to anoint David as king in place of Saul, who died. Unlike Saul, David gained God's favor, being faithful to God at all times (except later on in the matter of Uriah). God empowered David and gave him success in all that he did. David led Israel against the Philistines until they were no longer a threat.

## God's Covenant with David

After David had proven himself faithful under all conditions, God made with him an unconditional covenant. That covenant was again similar to those made by emperors in the ancient Near East. One category of such covenants was called "covenants of grant." If a vassal king proved faithful to an emperor under all conditions, then the emperor would make with him a covenant of grant. Such a covenant was a free gift, a token of the emperor's love for the vassal king. The vassal king became known as the emperor's "son," not just as his "servant." The emperor was called the vassal king's "father."

In covenants of grant, the emperor gave the vassal king (a promised) land or lands over which he and his heirs would rule forever. As in other covenants, the emperor undertook to protect the vassal king and his people in the event of a mortal threat. The emperor promised to annihilate a common enemy provided the vassal king remained faithful to the emperor. If a vassal king proved unfaithful, then the emperor would replace him with an heir who was faithful. By that means, the emperor would preserve the lineage and people of the vassal king.

Each of these features of ancient Near Eastern covenants of grant applied to God's covenant with King David. David was known as God's "servant" and "son" and God was called David's "father." God guaranteed David an unfailing line of ruling heirs to sit on David's throne as well as a land in which they could dwell. God promised to protect both king and people so long as the king remained faithful to God.

The opposite was also true. The king could lose God's protection for himself and his people if he became unfaithful. In an instance in which David sinned, for example, a plague killed thousands. As you can see, on the king of Israel hung Israel's welfare for better or for worse. The king now served as Israel's proxy, mediating with God in obtaining Israel's protection. Thus, although the covenant that God made with David was unconditional, the protection clause of that covenant remained conditional.

David, being a faithful king, became the means by which God delivered Israel from all her enemies. In fact, King David's reign commenced a golden age for Israel. David and Solomon, David's son, themselves became emperors over the nations of the ancient Near East. On the one hand, they acted as "servant" and "son" (as vassal) to the God of Israel. On the other, they fulfilled the role of "father" (of emperor) to the vassal kings of their empire, who acted as *their* "servants" and "sons."

God's covenant with David (the Davidic covenant) changed Israel's circumstances. Israel now no longer needed to keep the terms of her covenant with God (the Sinai covenant) to obtain God's protection. She was merely required to be loyal to her king. But this condition also meant that Israel's fortunes would fluctuate with her king's faithfulness or unfaithfulness. Instead of being a step closer to attaining the status of her ancestors, Israel now seemed a step further away. Instead of being herself faithful to God under all conditions, Israel left that up to her king.

Of Israel's kings who followed David, few were faithful to God. God replaced unfaithful heirs of David with faithful ones as long as he could find them. After King Solomon, Israel's condition quickly deteriorated. Jeroboam broke away from Solomon's son and ruled over the ten northern tribes of Israel. None of the kings of the Northern Kingdom was faithful to God. So few kings of the Southern Kingdom were faithful that within several centuries of Davidic rule all Israel was exiled from her land. Israel finally lost God's protection.

With the exile, Israel's circumstances changed again. Some of her people maintained their ethnic integrity among the nations of the world. Others assimilated into the nations and, like those nations, became known as Gentiles. God's covenant with

David, however, was unconditional. David would always have an heir or heirs ruling over the people of Israel and a land or lands in which they could live.

The prophet Jeremiah, who lived at the time Babylon destroyed Judah, reaffirmed God's promise to David. David's heirs, he predicted, would continue to rule over Israel forever—so long as there was day and night. Ezekiel, who prophesied at Judah's exile, predicted in an allegory that God would transplant David's heirs to other lands. There, in exile, they would rule over Israel and again gain renown. Perhaps these prophecies explain why some prominent royal families in the world today trace their lineage to King David. These prophecies also allow for the possibility that there are other lands of inheritance besides the first.

### God Makes a New Covenant

Isaiah picks up the threads of all the covenants God made and prophesies what their outcome will be. He predicts that God will again create special circumstances at the end of the world. Then, those who return from exile will once more keep God's covenant *as a nation.* As they prove faithful to God under all conditions, God will make with them an unconditional covenant (a covenant of grant). They will live to enjoy all its blessings during the millennial time of peace. They will be as Abraham, Isaac, and Jacob, their fathers.

According to Isaiah, God's new covenant will be a composite of all former covenants God made. It will contain all their positive features. God will make the new covenant with his people *as a nation,* like the Sinai covenant. God will give his people lands of inheritance as a free gift, as in his covenant with Abraham, Isaac, and Jacob. Their posterity will continue and increase through all generations of time and in eternity, even as he promised their ancestors. God will protect his people from their enemies, as under the terms of the Davidic covenant. He will endow them with his Spirit, even as God covenanted with the Levite priests. God will make the new covenant following a worldwide destruction of the wicked, as he did with Noah after the Flood.

In her distress in those days, Israel will give birth to another son—a deliverer—a faithful heir and descendant of David. God's servant or vassal will mediate God's covenant with Israel as Moses mediated the Sinai covenant. He will call Israel out of all nations to safety in Zion. God's people will be reborn as a nation in the "day of the Lord," as Israel was born at the exodus out of Egypt. God will exalt his covenant people before all nations as a testimony of what he can do for them.

# Chapter 5

# Zion and Babylon Ideologies

I have described some of the discoveries I made in the Book of Isaiah as I set myself the task of discovering its key. You can see why I was excited about them. They shed new light on Hebrew prophecy in general and on Isaiah in particular. However, the best discovery was yet to come. That discovery was William Brownlee's, a Bible scholar who had been studying the Isaiah document found among the Dead Sea scrolls. The Dead Sea scroll of Isaiah had peculiarities that led him to look for structural patterns.

Brownlee discovered that the Book of Isaiah consisted of two structured halves. Each half contained thirty-three chapters. In addition, each half divided into seven parts. The seven parts of the first half matched the seven parts of the second half in content. Brownlee believed this division to be merely a mechanical kind of structure. He presumed that the Hebrews liked to organize their writings in parallel fashion. He didn't attempt to analyze the structure. He simply noted its outline.

## Isaiah's Seven-Part Structure

I believe William Brownlee's discovery proved to be very significant indeed. However, he didn't live to realize that. A friend of his, R. K. Harrison, who was guiding my doctoral studies, suggested I analyze the structure for my dissertation. As I did so, I realized that this structure of Isaiah surpassed all others. It tied together everything I had discovered before and revealed a wealth of information I had never anticipated. It opened up an entirely new dimension of Hebrew prophecy.

I found that each of the seven parts in each half of the book possessed a pair of themes. The book's content was organized around them. These themes consisted of opposites: (1) ruin and rebirth, (2) rebellion and compliance, (3) punishment and deliverance, (4) humiliation and exaltation, (5) suffering and salvation, (6) disloyalty and loyalty, and (7) disinheritance and inheritance. The seven pairs of themes in the first half of the book matched those in the second half. The two halves thus closely paralleled each other.

This was a complex structure. Nothing like it appeared in all ancient Near Eastern literature. I concluded that it must have originated with Isaiah. But what did this configuration of prophetic themes mean? This was like discovering a new book of prophecy.

I knew that the Hebrew prophets organized their writings in parallels. In parallels, something is stated twice, the second statement varying slightly from the first. The Hebrew prophets made parallel statements in individual verses, and they even organized entire blocks of chapters in parallel, as in this case.

One special type of parallelism they used was chiasms. In chiasms, things are also repeated, but in reverse order, usually with a key idea in the center. Observe the **a–b–a** structure of the following verse, for example: "I have raised up one from the north –**a**–who calls on my name–**b**–who shall come from the direction of sunrise"–**a** (Isaiah 41:25).

I noticed that the first three pairs of themes of Isaiah's structure paralleled the last three in reverse order. They were a mirror image of each other. This structure was thus a chiasm. The key idea in the center was the paired themes of humiliation and exaltation.

1.–**a**–Ruin and Rebirth (Isaiah 1–5; 34–35)

2.–**b**–Rebellion and Compliance (Isaiah 6–8; 36–40)

3.–**c**–Punishment and Deliverance (Isaiah 9–12; 41–46:13b)

4.–**d**–Humiliation and Exaltation (Isaiah 13–23; 46:13c–47:15)

5.–**c**–Suffering and Salvation (Isaiah 24–27; 48–54)

6.–**b**–Disloyalty and Loyalty (Isaiah 28–31; 55–59)

7.–**a**–Disinheritance and Inheritance (Isaiah 32–33; 60–66)

Humiliation and exaltation were also the central themes of the first structure I had discovered. That structure contrasts a false god, the king of Babylon, with the God of Israel, the King of Zion. It illustrates how the king of Babylon exalts himself to high heaven, then falls, utterly humiliated. The opposite idea also appears. The Suffering Servant suffers utter humiliation before he is exalted as Israel's heavenly King.

I concluded that humiliation and exaltation had to be *the* key concepts of the Book of Isaiah. In one structure, Isaiah created archetypes around them—the king of Babylon and the King of Zion. In another, the most intricate structure of all, he organized all the book's content around them. Could humiliation and exaltation represent the two opposite final destinies of humanity?

## A Prophecy and a Theology

I noticed other things about the themes of Isaiah's structure. They seemed to suggest two ways Israel could go, two courses of action from which to choose. I tried to read into these themes what their configuration could mean. On the one hand, *humiliation*—a central theme—appeared to involve *ruin* and *disinheritance,* two parallel or matching themes. It also involved *punishment* and *suffering,* two additional matching themes. All seemed to be a consequence of *rebellion* and *disloyalty.*

74

The counterpart of each of these themes, on the other hand, seemed to interplay in the identical way. *Exaltation*—a central theme—appeared to involve *rebirth* and *inheritance*. They were connected to *deliverance* and *salvation*. And all seemed to be the result of *compliance* and *loyalty*. Evidently, this structure depicted what could or would happen to God's people as individuals or as a nation. It described two opposite causes and their effects. This was not just a prophecy—it was a whole theology.

But there was more to this structure than a simple configuration of themes. Within the structure itself, I found that Isaiah used numerous literary devices. Each of the structure's seven paralleled parts was a self-contained unit. Each had its own individual characteristics, making it unique. It was obvious someone had deliberately created this seven-part structure with uncommon creativity and skill.

I saw that the seven-part division helped establish important concepts. Each part conveyed a message of its own. That message was developed between the two paralleled blocks of chapters in each of the seven parts. Concepts were established piecemeal within each part of the structure, then expanded upon from one part to the next. What was developed in one became the starting point for that which followed. And so forth. Let's look briefly at the seven-part division.

## Ruin and Rebirth (Isaiah 1–5; 34–35)

The two paralleled blocks of chapters of part one establish the idea of a reversal of circumstances between Zion and the nations of the world. At some point, God's people will experience rebirth as a nation, revived from their deteriorated state. The covenant curses they have endured will be replaced by blessings. At the same time, the nations will suffer ruin, and their blessed state will turn into a cursed one. By means of literary patterns within part one, Isaiah shows that this reversal of circumstances occurs simultaneously for both parties, Zion and the nations.

Isaiah also shows that it is Zion that is born or reborn, not Israel. Zion is not all Israel. It consists of an elect group of people within Israel. Isaiah defines Zion as both a people and a place. Zion is made up of people who repent. Zion is also the place to which those who repent will return from among the nations, a place of safety for God's people at the time the nations are ruined. Isaiah includes, among the nations, those of Israel who do not repent. The setting for these events is both the "day of the Lord" and the end of the world—they are one and the same.

## Rebellion and Compliance (Isaiah 6–8; 36–40)

Part two of the structure maintains the concept of a reversal between Zion and the nations. In addition, it establishes the idea that Israel's rebirth as

Zion comes as a result of Zion's compliance with the terms of God's covenant. Many people go forward and prove themselves faithful to God under all conditions. When God puts Zion to the test, it passes. Those of Israel who rebel against God, on the other hand, bring upon themselves their own ruin. The rebellious fail the same test that Zion passes.

### Punishment and Deliverance (Isaiah 9–12; 41–46)

Part three of the structure maintains the previous concepts and builds upon them, showing how God intervenes to deliver his people from their cursed state. God raises up the king of Assyria to mete out punishment on the wicked who oppress them. The king of Assyria serves as God's instrument for reducing the unrepentant nations to ruin.

God also raises up his "servant" and "son" as an instrument for delivering his people. God's servant brings about Zion's deliverance by releasing God's people from bondage or exile, as Moses did in Egypt. He paves the way for God's repentant people—Zion—to return home from exile to the place Zion in a new exodus.

### Humiliation and Exaltation (Isaiah 13–23; 46–47)

Part four builds upon these concepts by establishing the idea of a new Babylon. Babylon is a composite of all that is not Zion. The nations of the earth, tyrants and oppressors, aggressive world powers, enemies and adversaries, proud kindred peoples, and the wicked and rebellious of Israel—all these and others make up Babylon. Like Zion, Babylon is both a people and a place—the world and its wicked inhabitants.

Isaiah's structure then contrasts Zion and Babylon, showing them to be opposites. Babylon exalts herself on her throne but is reduced to the dust. Zion, humbled in Babylon, rises from the dust to sit enthroned. When Babylon assumes an anti-Zion and anti-God posture, God intervenes to bring about the humiliation of Babylon and the exaltation of Zion.

## Suffering and Salvation (Isaiah 24–27; 48–54)

Part five goes still further to describe the reversal between Zion and Babylon in terms of salvation on the one hand and suffering on the other. God's repentant people are relieved of suffering as their enemies—Babylon—begin to suffer a full measure of covenant curses. Salvation for Zion consists of God's removing her sins, delivering her from distress, and turning her curses into blessings. Zion even overcomes the curse of death and attains a state of immortality. The God of Israel himself, the King of Zion, brings about these spiritual aspects of Zion's salvation. Isaiah's messianic theology finds its fullest expression in this part of the structure.

As God's people qualify spiritually, God's servant or vassal brings about the physical aspects of Zion's salvation. The servant's schooling of Israel in the law of the covenant, as Moses did, facilitates Zion's return from exile. God's servant acts as a model of righteousness both in keeping the terms of God's covenant and in proving faithful to God under all conditions. Salvation occurs for Zion when her people faithfully endure a period of pain and suffering. As God delivers his servant from suffering and empowers him, so God's servant delivers and empowers Zion.

## Disloyalty and Loyalty (Isaiah 28–31; 55–59)

Part six of Isaiah's structure establishes the idea of two covenants, a covenant of life and a covenant of death. With those who exercise loyalty toward him, God makes a covenant of life—an unconditional covenant. These obey God's word, as God's servant reveals it. They keep the terms of God's covenant *as a nation.* They respond to the servant's summons to return from among the nations. They prove faithful to God under all conditions.

Those disloyal toward God, on the other hand, alienate themselves from him and therefore make a "covenant with death." Those who do so reject God's word and rely instead on human counsel or schemes. They oppress the people of God and turn and fight against Zion. Among them are murderers, adulterers, evildoers, and hypocrites. For them, God's instrument of death is the king of Assyria, from whom God's faithful people are delivered.

## Disinheritance and Inheritance
## (Isaiah 32–33; 60–66)

Part seven establishes the idea of an eternal separation between the righteous and the wicked. One group receives a glorious and everlasting inheritance; the other suffers a shameful and everlasting disinheritance. The wicked include cultists as well as those in authority who exclude and persecute the righteous. The righteous include additional "servants" and "sons" of God, those who follow God's model of righteousness. These servants are among those who prove faithful to God under all conditions. They serve the God of Israel at all costs. They resemble God's righteous servant or vassal and assist him in delivering God's people.

Such examples of extreme wickedness on the one hand, and of extraordinary righteousness on the other, conclude Isaiah's development of concepts. They show that God's purpose is to lift his people to a higher spiritual and physical plane. They also show that such an ascent to a higher plane is actually helped by the opposition and adversity that extreme wickedness provides. A description of the opposite fates of the two groups, the righteous and the wicked, climaxes the structure.

## Structures Determine Time Frames

After I analyzed this seven-part structure for my doctoral thesis, I later published it as a scholarly book. Some of the structure's additional features appear in the following chapters. This structure creates an entirely new dimension for the Book of Isaiah, so that we can no longer look at the book from a linear, one-dimensional timeline perspective.

Isaiah's seven-part structure does not deal with events that happen over a long period of time—decades, centuries, or millennia—as some of the other structures do. Instead, it creates a *single* setting—the "day of the Lord"—at the end of the world for all the events Isaiah prophesies. In that respect, it resembles Isaiah's structure of recycled events that he links together domino fashion. That structure's setting, too, is the "day of the Lord" at the end of the world. However, it doesn't account for the book's entire content as this seven-part structure does.

This seven-part structure doesn't overrule or eliminate the validity of the structures that *do* deal with linear events over long periods of time, which structures are superimposed over it. The structure *trouble at home, exile abroad,* and *happy homecoming,* for example, is one such linear structure. Linear structures—which begin in Isaiah's time and end in the endtime—remain valid and are important. Together, Isaiah's several structures resolve the paradox of Hebrew prophecy, at least as far as Isaiah is concerned. They are an essential key to what otherwise remains a sealed book.

Just how does Isaiah's prophecy, in fact, relate both to Israel's past and to her future? How does it apply to ancient history and to the end of the world simultaneously? By establishing the endtime as the setting for the entire book, this seven-part structure helps to provide the answer.

First, *apart* from this structure we would conclude that the negative aspects of Isaiah's prophecy apply to the time of Isaiah himself. Those negative aspects deal with God's raising up the king of Assyria to punish his people. There was an actual king of Assyria in Isaiah's day who fulfilled that role. The linear structures accept that fact as a basis.

Second, according to this seven-part structure there will be a "king of Assyria" at the end of the world who will fulfill that role again. That agrees with Daniel's apocalyptic prophecy of an endtime king of the North. This time, however, the role of the king of Assyria will be part of an endtime scenario that will include God's deliverance of Zion. In this structure, the punishment the king of Assyria inflicts on the nations and God's deliverance of Zion occur simultaneously.

In Isaiah's day, therefore, mainly the negative aspects of Isaiah's prophecy were fulfilled while its positive aspects mostly awaited fulfillment at the end of the world. In the endtime itself, however, both the positive *and* the negative aspects of Isaiah's prophecy will be fulfilled. On that level, Isaiah's prophecy applies completely to the end of the world, just as apocalyptic prophecy does. On that level, in fact, Isaiah's prophecy *is* an apocalyptic prophecy. This structure makes it apocalyptic by creating an endtime setting for the whole book. In that sense, history will indeed repeat itself, and Isaiah's prophecy will have a double fulfillment.

To make that double fulfillment possible, Isaiah selects actual episodes of Israel's history—of events in his own day and prior to it—that typify the endtime. Isaiah uses these episodes of history as a basis for prophesying about the endtime. In addition, Isaiah was shown events that would soon occur in his day. Isaiah uses those events as a basis for prophesying both about his day *and* about the endtime. That manner of prophesying goes beyond what apocalyptic prophets do. Apocalyptic prophets name world powers and tyrants of their day that typify the world powers of the endtime. But they don't show them acting out their roles both in their day *and* in the endtime, as Isaiah does.

Isaiah accomplishes this two-dimensional manner of prophesying by using different literary structures. These structures make his particular style of prophecy possible. On the one hand, his linear structures begin with his own day and end in the endtime. On the other hand, his endtime structures both begin and end in the endtime. By using two different kinds of structures to establish two distinct settings—Isaiah's day and the endtime—Isaiah prophesies the future of two distinct time periods.

## Zion and Babylon as Archetypes

Isaiah's seven-part structure, however, accomplishes more. It reduces all humanity to two categories—Zion and non-Zion. It identifies Zion as an elect group among the people of God. These ascend from a lower to a higher spiritual and physical plane. They are reborn and exalted as the people of God at the time they return from among all nations. They are called by a new name—Zion.

The structure also identifies non-Zion by a new name—Babylon—those who alienate themselves from God, their Maker. In pursuing that course, they ultimately turn against God and descend to a lower spiritual and physical plane. Isaiah's prophecy of an endtime Babylon thus resembles John's prophecy in the Book of Revelation. John's endtime Babylon has the same character traits as does Isaiah's in this structure.

Isaiah's seven-part structure creates archetypes of Zion and Babylon, just as the first structure I discovered creates archetypes of the King of Zion and the king of Babylon. That, too, is what apocalyptic prophecy does. Apocalyptic prophecy teaches the doctrine of the two ways, of good and evil, making archetypes of Zion and Babylon. But it doesn't reach as far in its breadth and depth of vision as does Isaiah. Isaiah's writings surpass all prophetic writings in their scope of vision and literary skill.

Throughout Isaiah's structure, we encounter two contrasting worldviews. The structure spells out the doctrine of the two ways, as it develops concepts from beginning to end. On the one hand, loyalty to God and compliance with the terms of God's covenant lead to rebirth, salvation, exaltation, etc. On the other, rebellion against God and disloyalty to his covenant lead to ruin, suffering, humiliation, etc. Ultimately, all humanity chooses one of two opposite ideologies—Zion's or Babylon's. And, ultimately, all humanity experiences one of two opposite fates.

Babylon's alienation from God and her self-exaltation act as a refiner's fire for Zion. Babylon's oppression of Zion is the very manner in which God tests his people's faithfulness to his covenant. Will Zion respond to Babylon's lethal oppression by striking back in kind? Or will Zion serve God and wait patiently for him to deliver her? Zion may know that God has created these special circumstances so that he might reclaim her and bless her. God has sent his servant to instruct her in the law of the covenant and to serve as a model of righteousness.

Babylon and all who belong to her, on the other hand, cannot know that they are sealing their own doom. Their eyes are blinded by wickedness and idolatry. Their sickness is incurable. They are like the people of Egypt before Israel's exodus. In this, the endtime of the world, they have grown past the point of responding to an appeal for repentance. By infringing on Zion's rights, they are bringing upon themselves the curses of God's covenant with his people. As in covenants of grant, those who infringe on the rights of a vassal invite plagues or misfortunes to come upon themselves.

Zion's faithful endurance of oppression in Babylon actually brings about a reversal of her circumstances. In her pain, Zion will give birth to a son, a deliverer. Zion's seemingly hopeless plight is the very occasion in which God chooses to intervene on her behalf. In this, the "day of the Lord," God will do all he has promised. He will do so because Zion, for the first time in Israel's history, has kept the terms of God's covenant *as a nation* and proved herself faithful under all conditions. God is duty bound to come to the aid of his vassal and deliver her from a mortal threat. Babylon's threatening of Zion with destruction causes Zion's divine Emperor to annihilate her enemies.

Zion will ascend from the dust to sit on her throne. Babylon will descend from her throne into the dust. The millennial time of peace will commence.

# Chapter 6

# The Tyrant and the Servant

In Isaiah's seven-part structure, the two main human actors in Israel's endtime drama are God's servant or vassal and the king of Assyria/Babylon. One establishes Zion, preparing a people for the coming of their God and King; the other destroys Babylon–the very world he epitomizes and represents. Isaiah's structure contrasts these two human actors as powers of creation and chaos, respectively. One represents the forces of good; the other, the forces of evil. They resemble two arch-opponents pitted against each other. They are like Horus and Seth of Egyptian mythology or like a latter-day David and Goliath.

In Isaiah's structure, the king of Assyria/Babylon is a composite of several tyrant types of Isaiah's day. Although he is one man, Isaiah combines in him the roles and character traits of a number of evil rulers who came before him. Kings of Assyria anciently set the precedent for militaristic world conquerors from the North, which is a role he fulfills. In addition, the title "king of Babylon" demonstrates the religious side of this archtyrant. Babylon set a precedent for every kind of idolatry. Babylon's socio-economic system was based on the manufacture of false gods, the works of men's hands.

In contrast to Babylon, Zion's socio-economic system is rural and agriculture-based. This lends stability to a society, especially when that society comes under attack. In Babylon's materialistic system, the "many" (the manufacturers of idols) depend on the "few" (the farmers). That system makes Babylon's society unstable. Babylon is thus the opposite of Zion. Zion is like a pyramid that has God as its head cornerstone. By analogy with Zion, Babylon is an upside-down pyramid, unstable at its base. Babylon's structure is ready to fall as soon as its king comes to power and completes the pyramid, making it vulnerable to collapse.

## The Tyrant Conquers the World

But another dimension to the name *Babylon* exists. That is the idolatrous nature of the archtyrant himself. As the king of Babylon, he makes himself into a god, a false god. Being the ruler of the world he conquers, he demands the worship and allegiance of all humanity. Isaiah mockingly compares him with figures in Assyrian and Babylonian mythology. This archtyrant aspires to become a god, the supreme god of all other gods. He means to rule those on the earth from heaven above—from above the clouds. Isaiah uses elements from both history and mythology to give an idea of what that person will be like. In this manner, Isaiah creates the archetypal tyrant or archtyrant—the idol king of Babylon.

Isaiah thus combines in this person the character traits not only of the ancient kings of Assyria and Babylon, but also those of an ancient false god. If Isaiah were living today, for example, he might combine references to Adolf Hitler, Joseph Stalin, and Darth Vader. The future world dictator will combine the evil traits of various types before him. He will conquer the world by military force, brutally enforce his false ideology, and possibly rule the world from a space station. Yet, in spite of mythological allusions, this archtyrant is a real person. He will exist at the end of the world and actually do what Isaiah says he will.

But Isaiah shows up the king of Babylon to be a counterfeit of godhood. All that the name *Babylon* symbolizes is a counterfeit of what is good. In Isaiah's structure, this tyrant king functions as a power of chaos, not of creation. His works and acts are destructive throughout the earth. Instead of being a god who gives or saves life, he destroys countless lives as well as human habitats. He takes captive and tyrannizes those left alive. He reduces the earth to a state of chaos, as it was in its beginning. When his work of destruction is finished, the few who survive must commence a new civilization.

God's servant, on the other hand, functions as a power of creation. His works establish justice and righteousness in the earth, which are the foundation of all good. He saves from destruction those who repent, who renew their allegiance to God. He releases them from captivity and tyranny and leads them to safety in the "day of the Lord." After the desolation of the earth, he and God's people rebuild the ruined places. They commence a righteous, millennial civilization in which God reigns, in which God's law and word are kept by all.

Chaos and creation patterns in Isaiah's structure show that chaos will briefly prevail in the earth. Chaos will overwhelm the world as a consequence of wickedness. The king of Assyria/Babylon may burn up cities and destroy whole nations. He may plunder their wealth like a thief in the night. However, he is really acting as an instrument to bring these evil consequences to pass. He has one purpose—to rule the world. But God has another. This evil tyrant will serve God's purpose, and then he and his work will come to an end.

In all Hebrew prophecy, wickedness followed by destruction appears as cause and effect. God's people should not concern themselves about a man who would cause such destruction in order to gain the whole world. Nor should they be afraid of him and his vast and invincible armies. Instead, they should focus on the task at hand and serve God. They should repent of sins that are the cause of destruction. They should keep the terms of God's covenant so that God may deliver them.

God's people need have no fear, no matter how disciplined or well-organized are their enemies. No weapon designed to destroy them can hurt them, no matter how deadly. God is more powerful than them all. The king of Assyria/Babylon is only a tool. Though he rules from above the earth, though he makes himself higher than all, God will thrust his soul down to hell, to the very lowest pit.

God planned the destruction of the wicked from the beginning. He commissions the king of Assyria/Babylon and empowers him for the task. God determined beforehand to bring a new and higher creation out of the chaos left by the archtyrant. The earth itself, and all humanity, are on an upward path of progression that cannot be impeded. God has decreed the destruction of all who do not repent before time runs out. Before the millennial era begins, all wickedness and tyranny will be erased from the face of the earth.

**Personifications in Metaphor**

The endtime of the world will resemble the time before the Flood. It will compare to that time both in wickedness and in the destruction of life that follows. Isaiah calls the king of Assyria/Babylon by the names *Sea* and *River*. He likens him to a new Flood that overwhelms the earth. This tyrant is destructive like the mighty sea heaving its waves beyond its bounds or like a river that overflows its banks, sweeping all before it. He overwhelms the wicked and inundates their lands. He leaves nothing behind him but disaster and desolation.

*Sea* and *River* were the two names of an ancient Near Eastern power of chaos. In Canaanite mythology, that power of chaos, together with *Death*, represented the forces of evil. However, just as God parted the Red Sea by the hand of Moses, and as God parted the Jordan River, when it flooded, by the hand of Joshua, so God will subdue *Sea* and *River* at the end of the world by the hand of his servant. God will save his people from *Death* when they prove faithful to him under all conditions. His servant will deliver them from the agent of death—the king of Assyria/Babylon—as Moses delivered Israel from her enemies in the wilderness.

God chooses the king of Assyria/Babylon as his *rod* and *staff* to punish the wicked, not the righteous. He functions as God's *axe* and *saw* to hew down those who fight against his people. Isaiah likens the proud and arrogant peoples of the earth to lofty cedars and mighty oaks. He compares their cities to dense forests. He likens their nations to high mountains and elevated hills. All these are hewn down and laid low by the archtyrant. He strikes to the earth the unjust and idolaters of humanity to fulfill divine justice.

The king of Assyria/Babylon personifies God's *anger* and *wrath*. God's *anger* will be kindled against evildoers in the day of his blazing *wrath*, the "day of the Lord." In that day, this evil tyrant will wield power over the whole earth as a reward for wickedness. The king of Assyria/Babylon will come upon them as God's *vengeance* and *fury*, his *rage* and *indignation*. He is God's upraised *hand*, extended against evildoers. Like a sinister *ensign*, he rallies an alliance of wicked nations to assist him in conquering the world.

The king of Assyria/Babylon is the *voice* of the wicked, a *tongue* speaking perverse things against God and God's people. He opens his *mouth* insatiably like hell, swallowing up people's souls. His *lips* flow with wrathful speeches. He is the *scourge* of the wicked, a *yoke* around their necks. He is *darkness* itself. As a power of darkness, he causes gloom and misery and brings a veil of darkness over the whole earth.

These metaphors, describing the king of Assyria/ Babylon, express his character traits as well as the nature of God's justice. Isaiah's personification of these evil traits in the person of the archtyrant helps us to see evil from another perspective. God is not an angry God who wants to smite and punish people. He is a kind and loving God, gentle, patient, and long-suffering. Nevertheless, people's evil doing brings its just consequences. God has promised to deliver his faithful people from the threat of death. God therefore permits a wicked person–the king of Assyria/Babylon–to destroy and punish the wicked, those who threaten and oppress God's people. In that way, justice is done. People ultimately bring evil on themselves.

The metaphors Isaiah uses appear throughout his book. They appear in many instances where the king of Assyria/Babylon is not mentioned by name. In some instances, Isaiah identifies these metaphors with the king of Assyria/Babylon directly. In others, he does not. But he links them by means of parallels to metaphors that do. Typically, once Isaiah establishes an idea in one part of his book, it is relevant throughout.

This use of metaphors means that Isaiah has layered his book with many aspects of the endtime scenario that are not necessarily obvious. We as readers may detect these metaphors and read into them a second meaning. On one level, Isaiah describes God's anger being kindled, his hand upraised, his wrath poured out upon the wicked. People choose darkness instead of light. Their tongue utters lies and speaks against God. They are burnt up by the fire, cut asunder by the sword. And so forth. On another level, the words *anger, hand, wrath, darkness, tongue, fire, sword,* etc., describe the king of Assyria/Babylon. He personifies these traits. Isaiah is also speaking about him.

The same thing holds true for God's servant or vassal. Isaiah also describes him and his character traits by means of such metaphors. Some of these metaphors are identical with those that describe the king of Assyria/Babylon; others are not. The ones that are identical imply that there exists an arch-rivalry between the tyrant and the servant. The two compete with each other for people's lives and souls. The metaphors that are not identical, on the other hand, distinguish the servant as a power of creation, as an instrument of God's deliverance.

God's servant thus also appears as a *hand.* He functions as God's *right hand,* releasing Israel's captives and oppressed. He is an *ensign* to God's people to rally them to repent, to return home from exile. He is the *voice* of the righteous, God's *mouth* to his people. He is the *rod* and *staff* that wield power over the king of Assyria/Babylon. He is the *sword* of God, a *fire* that consumes tyrants.

Other metaphors describe the servant only. They apply uniquely to him. For example, the servant is a *trumpet* heralding the "day of the Lord," announcing God's coming to reign on the earth. The servant functions as a *light* lighting up the darkness. He personifies *righteousness* and *faithfulness* to God's covenant. He serves as an example of these character traits in a time of wickedness. God's servant is a chosen *arrow*, a righteous *branch* that bears good fruit. He is a saving *arm* of God, by whose means God intervenes in the affairs of his people to deliver them.

## The Servant Has Many Types

Like the king of Assyria/Babylon in Isaiah's structure, God's servant is a composite of ancient types. Isaiah combines in him the roles and character traits of a number of heroes of Israel. Although he is one man, he accomplishes at the end of the world what others did at different times in history. That is so because Israel's endtime scenario consists of a repeat performance of every major event in Israel's past. God doesn't choose several heads of his people all at once, each one fulfilling a leading role simultaneously. He chooses one righteous leader, as he did anciently, whom he empowers for the task.

Like Abraham, the servant comes from the east or northeast in relation to Israel. Like Abraham, he calls on God's name and is righteous and beloved of

God. As Abraham kept God's counsel and performed all God asked him to do, so does the servant. As Abraham was valiant in delivering his associates from the kings of the north, so is the servant. As God spared the righteous in Sodom for Abraham's sake, so God will spare those who repent in Babylon for his servant's sake.

Like Moses, God's servant is called a shepherd of his people. Like Moses, he intercedes for the transgressors among his people. Like Moses, he releases God's people from bondage and delivers them in an exodus to the promised land. As Moses led Israel's return wandering in the wilderness, so the servant leads Israel's return. As Moses mediated God's covenant and served as a lawgiver to Israel, so does the servant. As Moses anointed Aaron and his sons to be priests, so the servant anoints the people of Zion to be God's priests. Just as Moses' strength did not fail, so the servant's strength will not fail but he will fulfill all God requires him to do.

God's servant also resembles Joshua. Like Joshua, he leads Israel's armies against their enemies and destroys them. Like Joshua, he assigns God's people inheritances in the promised land. The servant further resembles Gideon. Gideon overthrew a vast Midianite army with only a few men of Israel. So God's servant will overthrow the armies of Assyria/Babylon. He will smash their *yoke* from the necks of God's people and break their oppressive *rod* and *staff.*

Perhaps more than any other hero of ancient Israel, King David provides a model for God's servant. The servant is a descendant of David the son of Jesse and a legitimate heir. God makes with him an unconditional covenant, as he did with King David. God chooses him and calls him his "servant" and "son." Like David, he is God's anointed one, filled with the Spirit of God. Like David, the servant overthrows the enemies of God's people and divides their spoil. As David led Israel's armies and united Israel's tribes, so does God's servant.

God appoints his servant as a *light* to Israel and the nations, as was David. God makes him a prince and lawgiver to the peoples of the earth, as was David. Like David, God's servant establishes justice and righteousness among the nations. In his day, peace will be established in all the earth. God's dominions will extend throughout the world, as they did in the days of David and Solomon, David's son. Like Solomon, the servant will grow renowned among the nations for his wisdom and understanding.

King Hezekiah, who lived during Isaiah's lifetime, provides another important model for the servant. In Isaiah's seven-part structure, Isaiah places the events surrounding Hezekiah's life in an endtime setting. These events, too, thus repeat themselves, with God's servant fulfilling the role of Hezekiah. For example, as Hezekiah suffered a mortal threat to his life, so does the servant. As Hezekiah poured out his soul to God in his deathly affliction, so does the servant. As God healed Hezekiah of his illness, so he heals his servant.

In Isaiah's structure, Assyria's siege of Zion or Jerusalem will repeat itself at the end of the world. As did Hezekiah, God's servant acts as a proxy of his people in obtaining God's protection. In the interim before Israel fully keeps the terms of God's covenant, she may obtain God's protection through the servant. Like Hezekiah, the servant intercedes with God for His people's deliverance from the besieging Assyrians. However, as they grow in righteousness and prove faithful to God *as a nation,* they will obtain God's protection themselves. The servant fulfills a temporary role on their behalf based on the protection clause of the Davidic covenant.

Others who typify the roles and character traits of God's servant include Isaiah himself. In his role as a prophet of God and a teacher in Israel, the servant resembles Isaiah. Like Isaiah, the servant accurately predicts the future, showing that God is with him. As God endowed Isaiah with a learned tongue, so he endows his servant. As God justified Isaiah when he met with opposition, so he justifies his servant in the eyes of all.

Like Job, whose sons and daughters were pleasure lovers, the servant suffers for the sins of others. Like David, whom Saul outlawed, the servant is numbered among transgressors. Like King Uzziah, who was covered with leprosy, the servant's appearance is marred beyond human likeness before God heals him. As God chose Cyrus and gave him power over nations and rulers, so he chooses his servant and gives him power over the nations and rulers of the earth. As God inspired Cyrus to rebuild Jerusalem and its temple, so he inspires his servant.

### Jewish Messianic Expectations

God's servant in Isaiah's structure thus embodies in one person all the positive features of Israel's heroes. Not surprisingly, the servant fulfills Jewish expectations of a coming Messiah. Of course, these expectations are not the same as those of Christians. Whereas the Christian idea of a Messiah centers around spiritual salvation, the Jewish idea centers around physical deliverance. Nonetheless, the Jewish concept of a Messiah has a valid basis in the Book of Isaiah, especially in Isaiah's seven-part structure. It also has a valid basis in the writings of other Hebrew prophets, such as Hosea, Jeremiah, and Ezekiel. The question is, is only one of the two concepts of a Messiah the legitimate one? Or are they both?

# Chapter 7

# The Ladder to Heaven

Isaiah's seven-part structure adds a dimension to Hebrew prophecy that requires a reevaluation of the nature of prophecy. At best, most scholars have been prepared to admit that prophets like Isaiah had the ability to make enlightened guesses about the future. But having published their erroneous positions, these scholars do not easily retract. It may take the fulfillment of Hebrew prophecy itself to convince these scholars.

On the other hand, scholars are undoubtedly correct in thinking that the Book of Isaiah could not be the product of just one man. However, neither could it be the product of several "Isaiahs" over several centuries. The many literary structures that bind the book's content together from beginning to end cannot be the result of many minds and perspectives.

The Book of Isaiah is not a patchwork, an accumulation of writings assembled in fits and starts. It is an intricately woven work of art, which required the highest literary skill to create—a masterpiece beyond the human mind alone.

## Isaiah—Prophet and Theologian

The book's seven-part structure requires that we give Isaiah credit for what *he* had to say about his writings. First, he claims that what he wrote are things he saw in vision. He saw and heard actual scenes of a future "day of the Lord." Second, he claims that what he wrote is the word of God. God inspired him to say it, though the prophet met with opposition for doing so. Third, he claims that what he wrote deals with the end from the beginning. To back up that idea, he structured his book around a complete and detailed endtime scenario.

Even if one doesn't accept Isaiah at his word, one must still give him credit for conceiving such a complete and detailed scenario. But why would a person go to such lengths to create this material for no personal reward? Does it not seem more reasonable to accept that Isaiah was, in fact, a man of God and that God was the author of what he wrote? For Isaiah to write with divine authority meant that the book was not his own concoction but rather is literally what he claims it to be—the word of God.

Nonetheless, if Isaiah limited himself to prophesying, one might still question his authority. In his seven-part structure, however, we find more than a prophecy. We also find a complete and detailed theology. Isaiah develops that theology incrementally, just as he does his prophecy. In Isaiah's Zion ideology we have already seen part of it. Keeping the terms of God's covenant brings special blessings and privileges. Proving faithful to God under all conditions brings even greater blessings and privileges.

### An Ascending and Descending Order

It is only natural, therefore, that Isaiah should divide people into ascending or descending categories, depending on their relationship to God. We may liken these categories to a spiritual ladder that ultimately reaches heaven. Those on any rung of the ladder may go up a step just as soon as they are willing and able to meet the conditions required to ascend. Those conditions have to do with covenant relationships. God has stipulated the terms of the covenants he makes with his people as a whole and with individuals. As the archtyrant's example shows, trying to take a shortcut to heaven can end in disaster.

On the lowest rung are those who follow the king of Assyria/Babylon's example of absolute wickedness, of out-and-out evil. Forming the next lowest category on the spiritual ladder are the idolatrous nations of the world and the rebellious of God's people. Above them are the people of God who do not as yet fully keep the terms of God's covenant. Above them are those who keep the terms of God's covenant but who have not yet proven faithful to God under all conditions.

Much of Israel's ancient history was confined to God's dealings with these lower categories of people. Exceptions were Israel's ancestors, Abraham, Isaac, and Jacob; Hebrew prophets, such as Moses and Elijah; and several of Israel's kings, notably David and Hezekiah. Isaiah uses these individuals as models of higher categories of spiritual progression. As mentioned, God's endtime servant resembles these prominent figures of Israel's past. He does so, however, not only in the roles he performs, but also in the degree of spiritual ascent.

Isaiah's seven-part structure, for example, depicts the righteous King Hezekiah as an exemplar of his people. He functions as a role model for them to follow. What he does, they do. By their common faithfulness to God, both king and people ascend up the spiritual ladder. These things typify what will occur in the endtime. The opposite also happens, for in the same structure, King Ahaz functions as a role model of rebellion. What he does, the people do. By their common rebellion against God, they descend down the spiritual ladder.

Isaiah thus connects people's actions to either righteous or wicked leadership at every level of their existence. People will follow a leader who is of the same frame of mind as they are, whether for good or evil. Unavoidably, the leaders of God's people play a major role in their lives, in the endtime as anciently.

## Passing the Tests of God

The Assyrian siege of Jerusalem in Hezekiah's day was an ordeal for both king and people. God orchestrated that event as a test of his people's faithfulness. By all appearances, they had only two choices: either surrender to the Assyrians and be deported to another part of the Assyrian empire, or be slaughtered by them. The huge Assyrian army that surrounded the city was well-armed and well-equipped.

However, every requirement for obtaining God's protection of his people under the terms of the Davidic covenant was in place. The people looked to their king for leadership as the king interceded with God for the protection of his people. Both king and people ignored the Assyrians' threats, trusting solely in God. They passed the test, so God destroyed the Assyrian horde in one night. In the morning, people helped themselves to the spoils of war. The Assyrian threat was gone.

Isaiah likens the people's reaction at this event to a Woman (Zion) who rejects an unwanted suitor (the king of Assyria). She laughs the Assyrian king to scorn, knowing that God, her husband, will protect her. Isaiah also describes how King Hezekiah sends messengers to the prophet Isaiah for help. To Hezekiah, the Assyrian siege is a tremendous ordeal. He is responsible for the safety of his people. Hezekiah likens their situation to a child ready to be born but whose mother lacks the strength to give birth.

Meanwhile, Hezekiah himself suffers a death threat through a plague or grievous illness. He experiences individually what his people are going through collectively when the Assyrians threaten their lives. As he pours out his soul to God, believing he is dying, God sends help. Isaiah heals the king and he lives on. Isaiah connects God's promise to save Hezekiah's people from the Assyrians to the king's agonizing ordeal. As God has delivered the king from death, so he will deliver his people. Hezekiah's suffering has paid the price of his people's deliverance.

Both king and people thus pass God's test. But God requires more of the king than of the people. The people are severely troubled and in pain over the Assyrian threat. What should they do to save their lives and the lives of their little ones? Can there be deliverance from such overwhelming odds? Coupled with that threat, moreover, the king suffers excruciating physical and mental anguish to the brink of death. Yet, he yields his life in willing obedience to God. He proves faithful to God under all conditions. The king's test is by far the greater.

In this manner, Isaiah shows how a deliverer is born. Like the tests passed by other deliverers, such as Moses and David, Hezekiah's test is severe. God has individualized the test for Hezekiah personally. His test is unique to himself, though it resembles those of others in its severity. Through this test, Hezekiah comes to know himself better. He is a better man for having passed through the ordeal. God did not orchestrate a test that would be too difficult for Hezekiah.

When he passes the test, Hezekiah himself is delivered. By passing the test he also becomes his people's deliverer. Furthermore, when his people pass the test—by remaining loyal to their king—they too are delivered. By passing the test, they are also born as the people of Zion or Jerusalem. Remaining loyal to their king in the face of a mortal threat demonstrates their loyalty to God. It shows that above all they trust in God to deliver them. Isaiah now identifies Hezekiah's people by the names *Zion* and *Jerusalem*. Both king and people have ascended a level.

Within the same structure, Isaiah then shows how Zion's or Jerusalem's role is to minister to Jacob or Israel. That lower category of God's people consists of those who have yet to pass such a test. God commissions Zion/Jerusalem (those who have passed the test) to do for Jacob/Israel what King Hezekiah has done for them. As they do so—as they prove faithful to God under all conditions—they will become like King Hezekiah. In Isaiah's structure, therefore, certain "servants" and "sons" of God, who assist God's endtime servant in delivering the people of God, ultimately emerge out of Zion.

## Living Role Models

Isaiah develops this theology of spiritual progression by means of literal persons and events of his day. Just as he does in prophesying the end of the world, Isaiah uses structures to develop important concepts. He demonstrates these concepts with actual characters out of history. It is a pity, therefore, and not a little surprising that scholars have not discerned Isaiah's endtime prophecy for what it is. Nor have they discerned his theology. What they have seen has been the exterior, the persons and the events themselves. On that basis, they have attempted to interpret Isaiah's writings and have missed the essence of what the persons and events represent.

In Isaiah's structure, the names of three children symbolize the following categories of people that we have identified: (1) those who do not keep the terms of God's covenant, because of disloyalty or rebellion against God; (2) those who keep the terms of God's covenant, but who have not proven faithful to God under all conditions; and (3) those who keep the covenant's terms and prove faithful under all conditions. These categories exist at the end of the world as well as in Isaiah's day. For each category of people, the "day of the Lord"—the end of the world—provides a test. Each thus experiences the endtime differently.

The first symbolic name is *Maher Shalal Hash Baz,* which means "Hasten the Plunder, Hurry the Spoil." By giving one of his sons that name, Isaiah is predicting the destruction and plunder of the Northern Kingdom of Israel by Assyria. The category of God's people symbolized by that name are those of Jacob or Israel who follow King Ahaz's example of rebellion. For them, there is no protection, either in Isaiah's day or in the endtime, when neither king nor people keep the terms of God's covenant.

The second symbolic name—of another son of Isaiah—is *Shear Yashub*. That name means "A Remnant Shall Repent" or "A Remnant Shall Return" (the verb *repent* in Hebrew also means "return"). This category of God's people are those of Jacob or Israel who renew their covenant relationship with God and keep the terms of God's covenant. Upon passing God's test, they become identified with Zion or Jerusalem. God commissions them to teach and instruct the next lowest category, so that they too may repent and return. Those who repent, who find themselves in exile, will return to Zion for safety at the end of the world.

The third symbolic name is *Immanuel,* which means "God Is With Us." In Isaiah's structure, that name represents those who keep the terms of God's covenant. In addition, they prove faithful to God under all conditions, as Hezekiah did. In that category are God's "servants" and "sons" of the endtime, who are deliverers in their own right. Like King Hezekiah, these servants minister to lower levels on the spiritual ladder. They bring God's repentant people to safety in Zion. God is *with* his "servants" and "sons," as he was with Hezekiah, to protect them and those to whom they minister.

Isaiah describes how God's endtime servants meet with opposition from those who constitute Babylon. God's servants suffer persecution and scorn at the hands of the wicked among God's people and of the nations. God's servants compete with idolaters, false prophets, evil authorities, and cultists for people's lives and souls. They mourn for the wickedness and injustice of God's people. They intercede with God in behalf of his people, and they offer an acceptable sacrifice to him. God spares his repentant people from destruction for their sake. He appoints his servants as kings and priests over the tribes of his people, giving them a new name to signify their ascent to a higher level. At the same time, those who persecute and fight against God's servants experience the fate of Babylon. They suffer a full measure of covenant curses and perish miserably.

Isaiah, and other Hebrew prophets, further distinguish the categories of people we have identified by the imagery of metals and stones. Precious metals and stones symbolize the category of "servants" or "sons." The semiprecious symbolize the category of Zion or Jerusalem. The common variety of metals and stones symbolizes Jacob or Israel. Levels below them are identified as dross and alloy. Like other metaphors Isaiah uses, we may read more than one meaning into them.

Those who survive the "day of the Lord" under God's direct protection Isaiah likens to gold, silver, and jewels. Those on the next lower level, like the Israelites in their wilderness wandering, God also protects from enemies. Nonetheless, they may be obliged to defend themselves against them, as the Israelites did. Lastly, under certain conditions God protects people for the sake of his "servants" and "sons," who serve as deliverers to those to whom they minister. For all other categories of people there will be no protection in that day.

In the millennial time of peace, gold replaces copper, silver replaces iron, copper replaces wood, and iron replaces stone. All society ascends a level. Those who remain in the lowest categories, who refuse to ascend, disappear from the earth. The earth will assume a paradisiacal glory. The earth itself then ascends a level also.

## Unimpeded Progress Upward

In Isaiah's structure, spiritual progression doesn't end with becoming God's "servants" and "sons." Just as covenant relationships govern every level of existence, so birth and rebirth continue to occur at every level of covenant keeping. Isaiah gives no indication that ascent up the spiritual ladder ever ceases. Rather, by giving examples of ascent (and descent) at every level, he implies that spiritual progression is an eternal principle.

Isaiah may not spell out the details of attaining the highest levels of ascent. No doubt, such details are sacred and are withheld from those on lower levels. They pertain to the councils of God and his holy angels. Nonetheless, Isaiah does spell out details of other levels. He shows how some do attain the level of God's "servants" and "sons," in the end-time as anciently.

In addition, Isaiah establishes the idea that those on higher levels minister to those on lower ones. Those above teach and instruct those below so that they may ascend to the next highest level. Those above serve as a model for those below to follow. Those above help and encourage those below and intercede with God on their behalf. At every level, God's love for his children is apparent as he makes provision for all. Only by their own disloyalty and rebellion do people cut themselves off from God's blessings and privileges.

Isaiah himself, for example, ministers to King Hezekiah, who is God's "servant" and "son." Isaiah is God's instrument for healing Hezekiah from a mortal illness. He serves as God's messenger to Hezekiah, bringing God's word to king and people. Undoubtedly, Isaiah was also a teacher to Hezekiah. Earlier in his prophetic career, Isaiah was himself ministered to by seraphs—holy angels who dwell in God's presence. A seraph healed Isaiah after he was struck dumb when he saw God. Beyond that, God, in person, commissioned Isaiah as a prophet.

By means of his seven-part structure, Isaiah reveals still more. He shows how God ultimately assigns *him* the role of a seraph, an angel of God's presence. After forty years of serving as God's prophet to kings and to their people, Isaiah ascends higher. He is admitted into the council of God. He is privileged to enjoy the same cosmic view that seraphs enjoy. He is henceforth to perform all the roles that a seraph performs. He ministers at the higher levels to God's people.

Isaiah shows how God's endtime "servant" and "son," too, ascends to the level of a seraph. Ultimately,

God's servant performs the roles that Isaiah or that a seraph performs. In that respect, the servant resembles Moses, who performed miracles in Egypt, or the prophet Elijah, who ascended to heaven in his physical body. Isaiah identifies the servant as the angel of God's presence. He delivers God's people at the end of the world as Moses delivered them out of Egypt. God's servant is as the angel of God going before the camp of Israel. Although he ministers to those on the earth, he himself is ministered to by God.

### Descent before Ascent

Lastly, in Isaiah's structure, ascent to a higher level is preceded by a temporary descent. That descent consists of the test of faithfulness God orchestrates for each individual. That test or descent involves a period of suffering and humiliation. It acts as a personal trial of one's faith. By means of that trial, a person learns more of God's character traits as well as his own. Ultimately, as one adopts God's character traits, one comes to know God himself.

The higher the level to which a person ascends, the lower or greater the temporary descent, and the more intense the suffering and humiliation. A person passes God's test by faithfully submitting to God's will, as Hezekiah did. As Hezekiah was born to new life by dying to himself, so may all God's children be reborn. Such rebirth occurs at every level of the spiritual ladder.

On the higher levels, selfishness plays no part in one's trial, as one suffers for others' sake, not for oneself. Exaltation on those levels carries that price tag, as one fulfills the role of deliverer to others. In each instance of ascent, the old self of the lower level must die so that the new self of the higher level might live. The old self must die even as the old generation of Israel died in the wilderness so that the new generation might inherit the promised land.

# Chapter 8

# The Savior-God of Israel

One who descends below all, and who ascends above all, is the God of Israel, the King of Zion. His saving mission is preeminent in the Book of Isaiah. His suffering and humiliation for others goes beyond anything anyone else has ever done. Scholars have called him the Suffering Servant of the Book of Isaiah. But Isaiah himself never calls him "servant." The word *servant* is used only in reference to God's endtime servant or servants we have just discussed.

Because scholars have applied the expression "Suffering Servant" to someone other than God's servant, readers are often confused about who is who. God's endtime servant is marred and then healed, but the God of Israel's suffering far surpasses that of his servant. If you analyze Isaiah's endtime structures, you can clear up this confusion between the two.

As I have noted previously, the structure that contrasts the King of Zion and the king of Babylon identifies the so-called Suffering Servant as the God of Israel. His descent, which includes his death, precedes his ascent as King of Zion. That descent and ascent are part of a pattern of humiliation and exaltation around which Isaiah structures his entire book. God himself sets the pattern for such descent and ascent. Those on lower levels of the spiritual ladder may ascend higher by following this divine pattern.

You will recall that humiliation and exaltation are the two pivotal themes of Isaiah's seven-part structure. They are also the pivotal themes of the structure that contrasts the King of Zion and the king of Babylon. According to these structures, exaltation is always preceded by humiliation. (Self-exaltation, on the other hand, is always followed by an enforced humiliation—as with the king of Babylon.) In the act of establishing the true pattern for exaltation, God—the King of Zion—suffers humiliation.

## God Is Bound by Covenant Relationships

A puzzling aspect of this reversal of circumstances, however, is that God himself should undergo such an ordeal. Cannot God, who is all-powerful, do what he needs to do without submitting himself to suffering and humiliation? Is God a mere mortal that he should suffer and die like a man? What is the point of that? The answer lies in the fact that God does nothing unless it is according to the covenant he has established with his people as a whole or with individuals. Within the bounds of covenant relationships we can resolve these questions.

Covenant relationships govern every level of existence on the spiritual ladder, whether higher or lower. The higher the level of ascent, the greater the saving mission of the one who ministers from there to lower levels. The higher the ascent, the greater or more effective is the service to lower levels. But the higher the ascent, the greater is the burden of suffering and humiliation that pays the price of deliverance.

Covenant relationships are binding upon God's people or individuals, but they also bind God himself. When God covenants to deliver his people from a mortal threat, he must do so as long as his people keep the terms of the covenant. Some examples include God's intervention in the days of Moses, Joshua, David, and Hezekiah. In each case, God delivered his people from enemies who were intent on, and capable of, utterly destroying them.

We have also observed that divine protection occurs on different levels of covenant keeping. On one level, God protects his people when they—*as a nation*—keep the terms of his covenant. On another level, he protects them by virtue of the righteousness of their king—so long as his people give the king their allegiance. In that case, the king must answer for his people's unfaithfulness to God. Upon interceding with God on their behalf, the king may suffer for their sake. He obtains God's protection for himself and his people in the role of a proxy. He keeps the terms of God's covenant in their stead, answering to God for more than himself.

We have further observed different kinds of divine protection. On one level, God protects his people though they are required to defend themselves against their enemies. On another level, God intervenes directly and destroys his people's enemies. Different degrees or levels of covenant keeping help explain these different kinds of protection. Keeping the terms of God's covenant merits divine protection. But proving faithful to God under all conditions merits direct divine intervention.

All these kinds of deliverance, however, have to do with physical protection against enemies. Whether in Israel's past or at the end of the world, it is the same. God is always willing to protect his people against physical enemies who threaten their lives. But the terms of God's covenant with his people go beyond such limited protection. Divine protection ultimately has to address death itself. God may deliver his people from physical enemies, but what happens when his people grow old and die? In that case, death has only been delayed for a time. They still die.

### Death, the Common Enemy

Ultimately, divine deliverance must consist of deliverance from *any* mortal threat. The king of Assyria/Babylon may threaten God's people, anciently or in the endtime. But what happens when that threat has passed? Aren't God's people then still vulnerable to death from other causes? In his love for his people, God has made provision to deliver them from *any* peril, including death.

According to Isaiah, the people of God will qualify for deliverance from death—for the first time in human history—at the end of the world. At that time, a nation of God's people, made up of individuals who repent of transgression, will renew allegiance to God. As the people of Zion, they will return from exile to the place Zion. They will keep the terms of God's covenant *as a nation* and prove faithful to God under all conditions. In their days, God abolishes death itself. They no longer die as mortals but live through the entire Millennium, and beyond.

As we have seen, ancient Near Eastern covenants closely resemble the covenants God makes with his people Israel. Understanding ancient Near Eastern covenants, therefore, can help us to understand the inner workings of God's covenants with Israel and with individuals. The emperor undertakes to annihilate a common enemy, provided the vassal king remains faithful to the emperor. A "common enemy" is one who threatens a vassal king with death. In God's covenant with Israel, then, if the common enemy is death itself, God is under obligation to come and annihilate death.

Just how God abolishes death is something we might consider. Death has always been a covenant curse. Death came as a consequence of Adam's and Eve's transgressing the law of God in the Garden of Eden. As with all others with whom God has dealings, God established a covenant relationship with Adam and Eve. As our first earthly parents, they consented to keep God's law, which included multiplying and filling the earth with their posterity. In the pattern of other covenants he makes, God blessed Adam and Eve with a promised land—in this case, the earth itself—and with an enduring posterity.

God gave Adam and Eve dominion over the earth, and its animal and plant life. God planted a garden in Eden that provided for all their needs. These things constituted the blessings of God's covenant. A singular restriction God placed on Adam and Eve was that they were not to eat of the tree of knowledge of good and evil. If they did—breaking the covenant—they would die.

God's covenant with his people Israel, therefore, actually provided a way for Israel to obtain a reversal of the curse of death. More than that, an entire people—potentially all humanity—could assume the deathless state in which Adam and Eve first found themselves. In that sense, the drama involving death would represent a gain, not a loss. All who would overcome death would actually ascend the spiritual ladder as a result of the adversity that death had provided. When death would finally be overcome, then those who had descended into death would ascend higher than they could have without experiencing death.

But how can an emperor annihilate a common enemy without actually conquering that enemy? Furthermore, can anyone overcome death without first being dead? On the other hand, can God, the Maker of all things, die? Wouldn't he then cease to exist as God?

Isaiah answers these questions in the structure that contrasts the King of Zion and the king of Babylon. There he introduces the idea of resurrection. Even as Babylon and her king descend from their thrones into the dust, so Zion and her King rise from the dust to sit on their thrones. In all cases, the spirit lives on with or without a physical body. It is only the physical body that dies and is resurrected.

But supposing God does, in fact, abolish physical death. Wouldn't people then still be vulnerable to die if they transgressed against God's covenant? If death was a covenant curse for Adam and Eve's transgression, then it is still so now or could be again.

Someone might again transgress the terms of God's covenant and introduce death a second time.

The solution to the problem is that God does more than conquer death. In his love for his people, he also takes upon himself their transgressions that are the cause of death. God assumes several roles in delivering his people, not just one. These roles apply to the highest apparent ministering functions on the spiritual ladder. They also involve the most intense suffering and humiliation on behalf of others of any delivering roles. God alone is actually capable of fulfilling these ministering functions for his people. No one else can fulfill them because all others are lower on the spiritual ladder. All others, to a greater or lesser degree, have transgressed the terms of the covenant.

### God, Our Proxy, Overcomes Death

In taking his people's transgressions upon himself, God assumes two kinds of proxy roles. These roles differ from that of an emperor. Both proxy roles, however, possess precedents in Israel's history. One of them, in fact, is the role of a vassal king who answers to the emperor for his people's unfaithfulness. By taking upon himself the form of a "servant" and "son"—the role of a proxy deliverer—God merits his people's deliverance from death itself.

In one sense, therefore, God acts in the role of emperor. God comes and annihilates death, a common enemy. In another sense, he acts in the role of a vassal king *to* an emperor. He answers for his people's unfaithfulness to the terms of the covenant, thus obtaining the emperor's protection for himself and his people. These dual roles are like the roles of those lower on the spiritual ladder. By assuming these roles, however, God accomplishes what no one lower than himself can accomplish.

The dual roles that God assumes introduce the idea of a rung higher on the spiritual ladder than the God of Israel. An emperor fulfills the role of "father" to his vassal kings. He is a king of kings and a lord of lords. A vassal king, on the other hand, fulfills the role of "servant" or "son" to an emperor, yet he is "father" to his own people. King David and King Hezekiah provide examples of these dual roles. The Hebrew prophets describe God as "father" both to Israel as a nation and to King David as an individual. But King David himself was "father" to those over whom he ruled.

Without actually calling God a "servant," Isaiah nonetheless assigns him vassal status. In the structure that contrasts the King of Zion and the king of Babylon, Isaiah shows the God of Israel being willing to suffer the prosecution and punishment that should be inflicted on a rebellious vassal. In several ways, however, Isaiah lets us know that this "vassal" is innocent of the crimes for which he is punished.

That situation represents an extreme example of a vassal king answering to the emperor for his people's unfaithfulness to the emperor.

By assigning vassal status to God, however, Isaiah implies that God—the King of Zion—answers to one higher than himself. The Hebrew prophets call that one the Most High God—El Elyon. Just as King David answers to God as a "son" to his "father," so God answers to the Most High God as a "son" to his "father." The God of Israel, in other words, is both a "father" and a "son." He is "father" to his people Israel *as a nation* and to individual vassal kings. At the same time, he is "son" to *his* father, one higher on the spiritual ladder than himself.

A second proxy role God fulfills on behalf of his people possesses a precedent in animal sacrifice. Under the terms of the Sinai covenant, if a man transgressed against God, he was liable to die as a covenant curse. But to forestall his death he could offer up a ritually pure sacrificial animal. The animal thus died instead of the man. It served as a proxy for the man. In theory, the man's transgression was transferred to the animal.

In reality, however, the sacrificed animal only symbolized what God himself would do. Proxy sacrifice for sin or transgression could have no human precedent. At some point, all humans transgress the terms of God's covenant in their mortal or cursed condition. No one has ever fully lived up to the ethical conduct God asks of his children. All humans, therefore, stand in need of God's deliverance from transgression and from its effects. We are not capable of delivering ourselves from our fallen state.

Neither can an animal be a real proxy for a man's sin or transgression, however ritually pure it may be. An animal, as a lesser species of life, cannot minister upward on behalf of one higher than itself. On Isaiah's spiritual ladder, those above minister to those below, not vice versa.

Consistent with his theology, Isaiah thus describes the Suffering Servant—the God of Israel—as a "lamb for the slaughter" and an "offering for guilt" (Isaiah 53:7, 10). Both ideas imply sacrificial death under the terms of the Sinai covenant. Isaiah then fuses this proxy role of animal sacrifice with the proxy role of a vassal king. In that manner, Isaiah establishes the concept of a proxy sacrifice *of* a vassal king on behalf of his people.

This concept applies appropriately to God's rung of the spiritual ladder. Only God can take upon himself his people's transgressions and reverse the effects of transgression. Those on lower levels cannot cause such a reversal. They can merely cease transgressing and keep the terms of God's covenant. Any other way of reversing the effects of transgression would destroy God's justice. God is bound by the same law of justice that he imposes on his people. Justice always requires that someone has to pay the price of transgression.

The multiple roles Israel's God assumes on behalf of his people parallel the multiple roles God's end-time servants will assume. God's "servants" and "sons," however, can merit God's blessings only within limited circumstances. They themselves depend on God for their deliverance. By fulfilling his saving roles, God brings about the forgiveness of sins, thus erasing the transgressions of his people. When their transgressions are erased, the effects of transgression may then also be erased. In that way, God introduces the law of mercy for all who cease transgressing and begin to keep the terms of his covenant.

By assuming these saving roles, God is able to abolish death permanently for his people. Moreover, in submitting to the will of his "father," he himself demonstrates faithfulness to God under all conditions. He serves—preeminently among all—as his people's exemplar. Being free from transgression, he nonetheless dies willingly for transgression. As an unblemished sacrifice, he suffers humiliation for the sake of his people. In response, God—the Most High God—delivers his "son" from death, a common enemy. But under those circumstances the only way he can do so is by resurrecting him.

As God himself, then, is delivered from death—by resurrection—so those who give God their allegiance may be delivered from death. Their deliverance results from a vassal king's proxy role on behalf of his people according to the terms of God's covenant. (The emperor is bound by covenant to deliver a faithful vassal king *and* those who are loyal to the vassal.) When Isaiah says that every knee will bow and every tongue swear allegiance, he identifies all who will be delivered from death together with their King.

By the same token, God reverses *all* covenant curses for his people, not only death. He does this by taking *all* their transgressions on himself. Death and resurrection are the most vivid instance of the reversal of the effects of transgression. Another example of such a curse reversal is Israel's return to the promised land. The land (Zion) will be restored and its temple rebuilt. The land will regain its fruitfulness and become as the Garden of Eden. God's righteous people (Zion) will multiply and fill the earth and enjoy its millennial peace. Sickness and fear will disappear. Sorrow will be replaced by joy. God's people will dwell in God's presence, basking in the bright ness of his light.

## A Reversal of Circumstances at the End of the World

According to Isaiah's endtime structures, this reversal of circumstances occurs at the destruction of Babylon and her king. Zion's covenant curses are reversed and she is blessed in the very moment

Babylon is cursed and falls. Zion undergoes a birth or rebirth at the same time that Babylon goes to her death. Zion's King comes to reign on the earth even as the reign of Babylon's king comes to an end. Zion's reversal of circumstances is thus directly linked to Babylon's.

At the time of that reversal, the righteous ascend a step up the spiritual ladder. Those who don't ascend to the level of Zion or Jerusalem perish with Babylon. God himself establishes the pattern for this ascent. His final exaltation as King of Zion completes a two-part drama. His prior humiliation as the Suffering Servant results in his exaltation at the end of the world. The king of Babylon, on the other hand, establishes the pattern for descent down the spiritual ladder. His final humiliation at the end of the world is a consequence of his prior self-exaltation.

Isaiah calls those who ascend and become God's "servants" and "sons" holy. These individuals prove faithful to God under all conditions. Above them are God's endtime servant and other servants in the category of seraph. These holy beings dwell in God's presence. Above them is God himself. Isaiah calls God the "Holy One of Israel." God sets the example of holiness. The seraphs praise him, singing "Holy, holy, holy is the Lord of Hosts" (Isaiah 6:3). His descent on behalf of his people—before his ascent as King of Zion—will ever remain an incomprehensible act of love.

# Chapter 9

# The End from the Beginning

As you can see, when I set out to explore the Book of Isaiah, I had no idea of the wealth that was really there. Who would have guessed that a prophet like Isaiah had layered his book with so many intricate structures? Who would have guessed that these structures held so many secrets, such profound truths? The literary features of the Book of Isaiah change one's whole perspective of Hebrew prophecy. Far from being a string of utterances by a prophet we could never properly identify (or by a number of unknown writers in a remote age), Isaiah's writings are vibrantly relevant to every living soul.

I didn't expect such a complete and detailed theology to be a part of Isaiah's prophecy. Nor did I really expect to find such a complete and detailed prophecy of the end of the world. In that discovery, I felt that I was more than rewarded for my efforts to relate Isaiah's writings to today. Certainly, I have not been able to prove indisputably that Isaiah speaks of our day. Nonetheless, I feel I have succeeded in outlining his endtime scenario.

With modern apocalyptic zealots, I could speculate about imminent developments in nations such as the former Soviet Union and the United States. After all, what Isaiah prophesies matches potentially what these nations are capable of doing. Isaiah does predict what is going to happen in our world at some point. I consider it fortunate that Isaiah's endtime scenario could be mapped out *before* it occurs rather than later. I leave it to the reader to decide whether that scenario could, in fact, develop out of present world events.

**A Polarization of All People**

Isaiah doesn't speak only of endtime superpowers who will fulfill their roles in the political arena—he predicts a great spiritual battle involving the king of Assyria/Babylon. This evil king or Antichrist, with his alliance of nations and vast armies, will make war on the people of God physically *and* spiritually. He will make himself the god of this world. Chaos-creation patterns in Isaiah's writings show the archtyrant will have the upper hand for a time. God will test the faithfulness of his people to the utmost.

Only in that way can they ascend higher on the spiritual ladder.

Many will be deceived by the sweet words of peace that the impostor will speak. His arrival on the world stage is one of the first things to occur in Isaiah's endtime drama. Those who believe him will be unwilling to suffer the temporary descent into humiliation that comes with being the people of God. Little do they know that they will descend anyway, most perhaps never to ascend again.

The fainthearted of that day will rob themselves of the holy Spirit that God gives to those who keep the terms of his covenant. Without God's light, they will be swept away by circumstances beyond their control. They will be left without hope of deliverance. They may even find themselves stirred up against that divine power that alone can save them.

All who fight against Zion in that day, from the king of Assyria/Babylon to the last apostate, will themselves perish. Those who gather under banners of hate and anger will be cut off from among the living. Those who scheme to gain control over the lives of others will fall into the very trap they have laid for others. Like all perpetrators of deception, they are not without blame. Their oppressive actions toward their fellow human beings reveal their rebellion against God.

A great polarization of the wicked and the righteous will occur at that time. People will be forced to choose to be either for or against God, as all middle ground vanishes. Their own choices will seal upon them their deliverance or their destruction. As God took Lot out of Sodom and the Israelites out of Egypt, as he delivered Hezekiah's people from the Assyrians, so God will prepare a way of escape for his people from the destructions that will come.

## The Literal Fulfullment of Prophecy

It has always amazed me that people could assume that the prophecies of the prophets might not be fulfilled. Prophecies of destruction, some say, can actually be nullified (in the sense of invalidated—not postponed) if people repent. They cite Jonah's prophecy of the destruction of Nineveh as an example. The people of Nineveh repented of wickedness and God did not destroy Nineveh as he said he would. Jonah became embarrassed and angry when God seemed to go back on his word.

The truth is that God *did* destroy Nineveh as he said he would—years later in the days of Tobit, as the Book of Tobit records. God fulfilled Jonah's prophecy to the letter. It just didn't happen when Jonah thought it should. One might further question how many people in the world today repent of wickedness as swiftly as the people of Nineveh did. With one accord, king and people completely turned from their evil ways.

Some people likewise believe that prophecies of a literal restoration of Israel can be explained away spiritually. They believe that many events predicted by the Hebrew prophets are not literal. The prophesied return of God's people from the four corners of the earth to the promised land; the rebuilding of the ruined places including God's holy temple; God's coming to dwell with his people as he dwelt with Israel in the wilderness—all these are just an allegory of things that have a mystical fulfillment. Their current theology doesn't make room for the literal word of God from another age.

As with the prophecy of Jonah, however, can anyone change what God has spoken? Surely, all that God has said will come to pass precisely as he said it. God himself keeps reassuring us of that. The prophets condemn all who contradict it. Is Isaiah's endtime prophecy, in fact, less relevant today than it was anciently? Rather, as the endtime approaches it becomes more relevant than ever before.

Similarly, can it be said that Isaiah's theology is less true today than it was in his day? With all that has transpired between Isaiah's time and ours, clearly it means as much to us as to anyone. If the life and sufferings of Jesus of Nazareth do not fulfill the major part of Isaiah's theology, then what does?

How does one explain away the New Testament theology that Isaiah has encoded in his book?

In addition, how does one explain away legitimate Jewish expectations of a Messiah? What about the Jewish hope of a Messiah who will restore the political kingdom of God? Will not someone come who will gather the tribes of Israel, unite Judah and Ephraim, and build the temple of God? If God's endtime servant will not fulfill these expectations, then who will? According to Isaiah and other Hebrew prophets, God will come in glory to a righteous people who have gathered out of exile to meet him. He will come to a temple that has been built to receive him. He will reign as King, in a kingdom that has been prepared for him. That work will be accomplished by God's endtime servant and those servants of God who assist him.

### Righteousness Precedes Salvation

In the Book of Isaiah, God personifies salvation. He exemplifies salvation and *is* salvation itself. (The name Jesus—Hebrew *Yeshua*—means *salvation*.) In like manner, God's endtime servant personifies righteousness. He *is* righteousness because he keeps the terms of God's covenant and proves faithful to God under all conditions. According to Isaiah, that is what constitutes righteousness, and it thus enables him to act as an exemplar of righteousness. The Dead Sea scrolls community recognized these personifications of God's attributes in the Book of Isaiah. According to Isaiah, *salvation* comes only after *righteousness* is established; *righteousness* precedes *salvation*.

There are two simple ways to explain this language of Isaiah:

First, God will come to save his people (from the king of Assyria/Babylon and from death) when they become righteous. He is bound to deliver them when they keep the terms of his covenant and prove faithful to him under all conditions. According to Isaiah, righteousness involves ministering to those in need. God's righteous people feed the hungry and clothe the naked. They plead the cause of the widows and fatherless. They stand up for the oppressed and release them from bondage. Righteousness means living a godlike life, living up to God's standard of righteousness, not our own.

Second, God's endtime servant acts as an example of covenant keeping and faithfulness to God. Like King Hezekiah, he serves as a model of righteousness that people may follow. As a result of his righteous ministry, other "servants" and "sons" of God emerge from among God's people. Through his servants in every age, God provides a pattern of upright living and ministering to others. When the servant's work of preparing a people of God is accomplished, then God comes. The servant is a forerunner of God's coming.

One of the reassuring things about Isaiah's end-time scenario is that everything will follow the pattern of the past. God will do only the kinds of things he has done before. We may recognize something as divine if it follows God's pattern. Counterfeits will abound, but something about each counterfeit will betray itself. Jesus said that if it were possible even the elect would be deceived. However, the elect will not be deceived, for they have learned the ways of God that helped them to pass God's tests. Those who are deceived are not the elect.

By Isaiah's definition, the elect are God's "servants" and "sons." These gather to Zion at the end of the world. Many of these servants will attain the seraph level of the spiritual ladder. In that way, God empowers them to gather his people from exile to Zion through all hostile elements—fire, water, and wilderness.

John identifies God's servants as twelve thousand of each tribe of Israel. They receive God's protective seal before the destructions of the endtime commence. Obadiah describes God's servants as "saviors on Mount Zion." On Mount Zion, he predicts, God will provide deliverance in the "day of the Lord." Daniel calls God's servants "saints of the Most High" God. They minister in the kingdom that God establishes on the earth at the end of the world.

In reading the writings of Isaiah in the light of his endtime structures, I wonder at the rapid ascent of

God's people that occurs in the endtime. The "day of the Lord" and the time just before it provide a rapid succession of tests for everyone. All people either ascend or descend. They have to. Into that brief time span is compressed every major test that God's people have faced before. Everyone will be either passing or failing God's tests. No one will stand still.

We should not underestimate the gravity of that day. Allegories like the wheat and the tares, the sheep and the goats, and the wise and foolish virgins alert God's people to the divisive nature of the endtime. The apocalyptic doctrine of the two ways will then be fully realized. The same special circumstances that will make angels of some men will make devils of others. Isaiah contrasts God's (unconditional) covenant of life with the covenant of death that some choose instead.

Isaiah further uses the imagery of tithing to show the division that will occur in the "day of the Lord." Those who escape destruction in that day will be but a tenth of God's children, called the "tenth of the Lord." Those whom God protects directly will be a tenth of the tenth. (Anciently, the people of Israel paid a tenth of their increase to the Levites. The Levites paid a tenth of what they received to the priests. That tenth of the tenth was called the "holy portion.") One kind of protection applies to those who keep the terms of God's covenant. Another applies to those who prove faithful to God under all conditions. Isaiah describes the latter group as "holy."

## Distinct Roles of Men and Women

By drawing on examples in Israel's history, Isaiah makes clear what God expects of men in that day. God's endtime servant will fulfill many of the roles that Israel's heroes fulfilled. God's servants who assist him will perform many similar saving roles. All these roles, however, have to do with men. Some, therefore, rightfully ask what roles God expects of women. Some go so far as to assert that the prophets are male chauvinists in their approach to life. Some claim that the few female role models in Israel's history are evidence of that.

Such thinking, however, misses the essence of what prophets like Isaiah teach. That there are few female role models among Israel's heroes is true. On the other hand, that is not the only source for the female role model. Because God does not give the lead to women doesn't mean that God or his prophets are male chauvinists. It does mean that God is more protective of women. Women have an intuitive sense of God's righteousness, which men have difficulty learning. Many recognize the falseness of Babylon and seek to cultivate an environment of Zion.

God therefore preserves the women from many of the hazards to which he subjects the men. Men may be saviors but women are those saved. God's covenants with his people and with individuals define distinct roles for men and women. There exists no protection for men or women except within covenant relationships. Keeping the terms of God's covenants and proving faithful to God alone will bring deliverance. Women, by their caring example, have much to teach men in that respect.

Isaiah, in fact, spells out the roles God expects of women. By fulfilling those roles, women ascend the spiritual ladder. Throughout the Book of Isaiah appear references to Zion as a woman, not as a man. She personifies God's righteous people allegorically. But she is also the role model of the individual woman. The things she does set a pattern for all women. They cover all aspects of her life, good and evil. I can give only a partial outline here.

Like everyone who ascends the spiritual ladder, the woman Zion repents of her transgressions of the terms of God's covenant. She faithfully endures the curses of the covenant that are a result of transgression. Her afflictions are like the term of her pregnancy. As the "day of the Lord" approaches, she travails with child. She gives birth to a son, a deliverer. She nurses him and cares for him until he is of age.

In the "day of the Lord," her son delivers her from the tyrannical king of Assyria/Babylon (and from other threats to her life). He leads her to safety under God's marriage canopy. God preserves her under his protective cloud of glory. God reclaims her by an unconditional covenant. He turns her curses into blessings. She forgets the shame of her youth and the reproach of her widowhood. She gives birth to a nation of children. She sits enthroned, clothed with power, and expands her dominions. She binds to her the children who return to her as a bride adorns herself with jewels. She who was banished, exiled, bereaved, and barren, now sings with joy at her numerous offspring.

From this symbolic imagery we observe that the woman gives birth to the man. Her role within God's covenant is to empower him to perform his role as deliverer. The man delivers her because she looks to him to do so. He measures up to her rightful expectations because she expresses abundant confidence in him. Here are patriarchy and matriarchy at their best. The one is not without the other. Both man and woman ascend together as they fulfill their respective roles—he of "father," she of "mother," he as husband, she as wife.

Theirs is a theology of ascent. They ascend together, recognizing each other's uniqueness. No competition exists between them, only harmony. Their children benefit when they fulfill their individual roles. They are as a king and queen of their posterity. God ever protects them and theirs according to the terms of his covenant. They receive a f  ,ess of joy as they follow God's pattern for male  .d female. God has created them in his own im  -male and female. They are born or reborn or  ↄ higher levels of the spiritual ladder as both m  and female.

Another question  ple ask is whether the role of deliverer or savi  .at God expects men to fulfill detracts from hi  ⋅n divine role. God's function as a deliverer ⋅  savior of his people applies on a much high  .evel of the spiritual ladder. All deliverers or saviors on levels below God, in fact, rely on God to do the actual delivering. God's servants can perform only roles that *qualify* them for God's deliverance. Their test is to exercise faith in God that he will deliver them.

By fulfilling the roles of "sons" and "fathers," of "daughters" and "mothers," God's people follow the divine pattern. God has provided covenant relationships within which his people may ascend. They grow into higher functions on the spiritual ladder by doing the kinds of things God does. God himself sets the pattern for ministering to lower levels, for helping those in need. As they follow God's loving example, they acquire his divine attributes.

## A Brief Warning before the End

The endtime is quite brief for so many things to transpire. Daniel and John speak of God's judgments in the endtime as lasting three-and-a-half years. Isaiah predicts three years of calamity, preceded by a similar period of warning. For three years, Isaiah serves warning that Assyria will subjugate Egypt. Then his prophecy is fulfilled. Similarly, in Isaiah's seven-part structure, God gives Babylon a three-year lease of time in which to repent. God gives ample warning of what he will do. These things typify Isaiah's end-time scenario.

Like Isaiah, God's endtime servant commences his mission *before* the "day of the Lord." God calls him as he called Isaiah to warn his people of coming calamities. As a result of the servant's mission, many will be stirred up to repent of transgression and renew their covenant relationship with God. However, others will harden their hearts. They will not believe that the times have changed. They will scoff at God's servants and hold fast to what is doomed to pass away. Isaiah likens such people to followers of ashes. They illuminate with mere sparks. They reject the *light* God sends to light up their darkness. By so doing they unwittingly reject God.

For those who repent, on the other hand, the "day of the Lord" will mean deliverance—deliverance from every evil, including death. God comes in that day both to avenge and to reward. He will avenge his people with the instruments of his vengeance. He will reward them according to their righteousness.

Those who ascend the spiritual ladder and acquire God's attributes will meet God and behold his face. They will accomplish what Moses sought to do for Israel and could not. They will fulfill all that Isaiah saw in vision. They will serve as a testimony that God foreordained the end from the beginning.*

---

*For the detailed textual analysis of the Book of Isaiah—on which this book is based—including an analysis of the book's structure, rhetoric, and typology, I refer the reader to my book *The Literary Message of Isaiah* (see Introduction, p. 10).

# Key Words

Abraham, Adam and Eve, Ahaz, Alienation from God, Allegiance to God, Allegory, Alliance of Nations, Ancestors, Ancient Near East, Ancient Near Eastern Covenants, Ancient Near Eastern Literature, Angel of God's Presence, Angels, Anointed One, Antichrist, Apocalypse, Apocalyptic, Apocalyptic Prophecy, Apocalyptic Writings, Apostasy, Archetypes, Archtyrant, Arm of Flesh, Arm of God, Ascent, Assimilated Israel, Assimilated Lineages, Assimilation, Assyria, Assyrians, Babylon, Babylon Ideology, Babylonian, Babylonians, Bible, Bible Scholars, Biblical Prophecy, Birth of Deliverer, Blessings of Covenant, Bondage, Book of Daniel, Book of Isaiah, Book of Tobit, Calamity, Canaanite, Canaanites, Captivity, Cause and Effect, Chaos, Chaos and Creation, Character Traits, Chiasm, Christian, Christian Theology, Christians, Chronology of Future Events, Classical Prophecy, Cloud of Glory, Code Names, Common Enemy, Compliance, Composite Types, Conditional Covenant, Core Ideas, Cosmic Vision, Council of God, Covenant, Covenant Blessings, Covenant Curses, Covenant of Grant, Covenant Relationship, Covenant Terms, Creation, Creation and Chaos, Cult, Cultists, Current Events, Curses of Covenant, Cyclical History,

Cyrus, Daniel, David, David and Goliath, Davidic Covenant, Day of the Lord, Dead Sea Scrolls, Death as Common Enemy, Deliverance, Deliverance of Zion, Deliverer, Deliverers, Descendants, Descent, Descent before Ascent, Desolation of Earth, Destiny, Destruction, Dictator, Disinheritance, Disloyalty, Dispossession, Divine Attributes, Divine Intervention, Divine Protection, Doctrine, Doctrine of Two Ways, Doomsday, Double Fulfillment, Effects of Transgression, Egypt, Egyptian, Egyptians, Elders of Israel, Elect, Elijah, Emperor, Emperor as Father, Ends of the Earth, Endtime, Endtime Scenario, Endtime Structures, Ephraim, Esau, Ethnic Israel, Ethnic Lineages, Evil, Exaltation, Exemplar of Righteousness, Exile, Exodus, Ezekiel, Faithful under All Conditions, Faithfulness to God, False Brethren, False God, False Peace, False Prophets, Father, Father as Emperor, Fathers, Female Role Model, Flood, Forces of Evil, Forces of Good, Foreordination, Forgiveness of Sins, Fulfillment of Prophecy, Future Events, Garden of Eden, Gentiles, Gideon, God, God of Israel, Golden Age, Good, Governing Structures, Greece, Harlot, Hebrew Bible, Hebrew Prophecy, Hebrew Prophets, Hell, Heroes of Israel, Hezekiah, Historical, History, Hittite, Hittites, Homecoming, Homeland, Horus and Seth, Hosea, Humiliation, Ideology, Idolaters, Idolatry, Immanuel, Immortality, Individualism, Inheritance, Injustice, Instrument of God, Intercession, Interpretation, Isaac, Isaiah, Israel, Israelites, Jacob, Jebusite, Jebusites, Jeremiah, Jerusalem, Jesus Christ, Jewish, Jewish Theology, Jews, Job, John the Revelator, Jonah, Jordan River, Joshua, Judah, Judaism, Judges, Judgment, Judgments, Justice, Key Concepts, King David, King of Assyria, King of Babylon, King of the North, King of Zion, Kingdom of Israel, Kings, Ladder to Heaven, Lamb of God, Land of the North, Lands of Inheritance, Last Days, Latter Days, Law of Covenant, Law of Mercy, Lawgiver, Laws of God, Levels of Covenant Keeping, Light to the Nations, Linear Structures, Linking Ideas, Literary Analysis, Literary Devices, Literary Features, Literary Message, Literary Patterns, Literary Structures, Literature, Lost Tribes of Israel, Loyalty, Malachi, Male Role Model, Marriage

Canopy, Melchizedek, Messages from Structures, Messenger of God, Messiah, Messianic Expectations, Metaphor, Midianites, Militaristic Superpower, Military Force, Millennial Civilization, Millennial Peace, Millennium, Ministering Functions, Model of Rebellion, Model of Righteousness, Mortal Threat, Moses, Mount Sinai, Mount Zion, Multiple Roles, Myth, Mythology, Nationalism, Nations of the Gentiles, New Covenant, New Jerusalem, New Testament, New Testament Theology, Noah, Obadia, Offspring, Old Testament, Opposite Ideologies, Oppression, Orchestration of History, Paradigm, Paradise, Paradisiacal Glory, Paradox of Prophecy, Parallelism, Passover, Patriarchs, Patriarchy and Matriarchy, Pattern of Prophecy, Period of Warning, Persecution, Persia, Personifications in Metaphor, Pharaoh, Philistines, Pilgrimage, Pilgrimage to Zion, Plagues, Plan of God, Poetry, Polarization of People, Political Authorities, Political Powers, Posterity, Power of Chaos, Power of Creation, Power of Darkness, Power of Light, Precedents as Types, Precious Metals and Stones, Pregnancy of Woman Zion, Price of Transgression, Priests, Promised Land, Prophecy, Prophetic Patterns, Prophetic Vision, Prophets, Protection, Protection Clause of Covenant, Proxy, Proxy Role, Punishment, Pyramid Structure, Rebellion, Rebellious of Israel, Rebellious Vassal, Rebirth, Rebuilding of Ruins, Redemption, Red Sea, Refiner's Fire, Reinheritance, Religion, Religious Authorities, Repentance, Restoration, Resurrection, Return from Exile, Revelation of John, Reversal of Circumstances, Rhetoric, Rhetorical Links, Righteous, Righteousness, Role Model, Ruin, Sacrifice, Sacrificial Animals, Safe Place, Saints of the Most High, Salvation, Samuel, Saul, Savior-God of Israel, Saviors on Mount Zion, Scrolls, Sealed Book, Second Coming, Second Isaiah, Seers, Self-exaltation, Separation of Righteous and Wicked, Sequence of Future Events, Seraph, Seraphs, Servant, Servant as Vassal, Servants, Seven-part Structure, Sinai Covenant, Sinai Wilderness, Sinuhe, Socio-political Condition, Sodom and Gomorrah, Solomon, Son as Vassal, Song of Salvation, Special Circumstances, Spirit of God, Spiritual Ascent, Spiritual Blindness, Spiritual Ladder,

Spiritual Progression, Spiritual Salvation, Structures, Suffering, Suffering Servant, Superimposed Structures, Superpowers, Symbolic Imagery, Symbolism, Temple, Temple at Jerusalem, Temporal Salvation, Ten Tribes of Israel, Terms of Covenant, Tests, Text, Textual Analysis, Themes, Theologian, Theology, Theology of Ascent, Thief in the Night, Threats, Tithing of People, Transgression of Covenant, Trial of Faith, Tribes of Israel, Trumpet of God, Twelve Tribes of Israel, Types, Typology, Tyranny, Tyrant, Tyrants, Unconditional Covenant, Unfaithfulness to God, Universalism, Uzziah, Vassal, Vassal as Servant, Vassal as Son, Vassal Kings, Vision, Visionaries, Wandering in Wilderness, War, Warnings, Wicked, Wickedness, Wilderness, Woman Imagery, Woman in Travail, Word of God, World Conquerer, World Powers, Worship, Zechariah, Zion, Zion Ideology.